LIFE IN RE

poetry Pt today

LIFE IN RHYME

Edited by
Rebecca Mee

First published in Great Britain in 1999 by Poetry Today, an imprint of
Penhaligon Page Ltd, 12 Godric Square, Maxwell Road, Peterborough. PE2 7JJ

A Catalogue record for this book is available from the British Library

ISBN 1 86226 586 0

Typesetting and layout, Penhaligon Page Ltd, England
Printed and bound by Forward Press Ltd, England

Foreword

Life In Rhyme is a compilation of poetry, featuring some of our finest poets. The book gives an insight into the essence of modern living and deals with the reality of life today. We think we have created an anthology with a universal appeal.

There are many technical aspects to the writing of poetry and *Life In Rhyme* contains free verse and examples of more structured work from a wealth of talented poets.

Poetry is a coat of many colours. Today's poets write in a limitless array of styles: traditional rhyming poetry is as alive and kicking today as modern free-verse. Language ranges from easily accessible to intricate and elusive.

Poems have a lot to offer in our fast-paced 'instant' world. Reading poems gives us an opportunity to sit back and explore ourselves and the world around us.

Contents

The Devil's Brew

It is called the Devil's brew
Alcohol is its name,
Just see the damage it can do
Like all drugs it treats us the
Same.

Slowly working around the body
Affecting the liver and heart,
Don't you know it has no pity
On what it tears apart.

It likes to cloud our mind
Making us act like fools,
It has no care what it leaves
Behind
It does not abide by any rules.

Jennifer Bell

Owed To My Father

My Father was born in Ireland in the year eighteen eighty five
He had to work hard all his life in order to survive,
So long as he could feed his family and have enough to pay the rent
He never was envious of others and was really most content.
I always loved, when he was at home, as he gave us 'Quality Time'
He's d sit us on his knee and sing or say a Nursery rhyme
Just to sit before a big fire on our shabby settee
I'd snuggled up to him and he would put his arm around me.
I'd listen to his stories and he'd play for hours on end
He'd listened patiently to me . . . he was my comforter . . . my best friend.
As I grew up I learned to appreciate him even more
His valuable advice helped me more times than I can score.
He never raised his voice to me though he could be quite stern.
And he taught me many lessons that at school I'd never learn.
To always treat other people as you would like them to treat you
Always to tell the truth and to be honest and be true.
If he had nothing good to say of anyone then he'd say nothing at all
In fact he was a giant among men though he was only five foot tall.
He had no special powers or obvious gifts to show
But if anyone needed help he was unable to say 'No'
He had left school at fourteen with no further education
So he had no certificates or any other qualification.
What he did have was a Christlike love of all his fellowmen
He'd been reared in a little town where everyone was your friend
He always had a ready smile and a 'Hello' for everyone
And a twinkle in his eye to match his super sense of fun.

He died at the age of seventy-three . . . thirty years ago last year
But when I am in trouble I can still sense his presence here,
I can recall his funny songs and the stories that he told
So I owe a lot to my late Father, a wee man with a heart of gold!

Mary Anne Scott

Searching

I'm searching for you everywhere
I can't understand why you're not there
In the distance you're ahead of me
When I reach you someone else I see

I'm at the hotel where we stay
So happy to be on holiday
Why can't I find you again
I ask but no one knows your name

Surrounded by our many friends
The feeling of well-being ends
Their faces show shock and pain
When I ask where you are again

I hurriedly open the garden gate
Sorry to be getting home late
I unlock the door, call out your name
There's no reply from you again

Am I asleep or am I awake
Why can't I stop this for pity's sake
I know that you're forever gone
But these constant dreams of searching goes on

Joyce Atkinson

My Space Is Filled

I bring her daisies for her hair, lilies for her bed
        The finest rose does match her cheek
An orchid spray and a ruby red
        A silver chalice fits her hand, like ivory, pale, so fine
Her heart is filled with love and care
        I feel it tremble next to mine
I turn just slight and see her face
        Resplendent, slender and with grace
Nought now could tempt me change my place
        She fills to full my needful space.

G Hodson

'Our' Lake District

One dreams of tranquil waters, hills and paths,
of snowcapped mountains and rugged stone walls
that look like shelves.
'Tis Wordsworth country for me and thee
to view the nodding wild daffodils beneath
the skeletons of the lowland trees.

We travelled to this unknown treat
with the Queen of Merrow* in the driving seat,
no planned route or bodyguard at hand.
She knew the pristine sites and places
that would put delight upon our faces.

From rugged bridges, mountain streams
to quaint old villages and bookshops
with their postcard views
to stops for coffee and a chew
'Tis a place to come again, I say
for there's plenty more for us to do.

Who is this Lady of the Lakes,
who drives the roads and lanes without mistake?
Her knowledge she reveals, we're told,
is better than an Ordnance Survey map
complete with all its folds.
Our home is a hotel across one lake
both by the name of Derwentwater they do relate.

From our window on the second floor
I gaze in wonder and in awe
across the shimmering water to the distant shore
at Helvellyn more sinister than those before
and at the green and pleasant land
all these set before me by God's almighty hand.

These pencilled words of our first visit
are written with one bought at Cumberland's of Keswick
a craft to which I can relate for as a Printer
and like the Lady of the Lakes, its books
and words on paper that we both appreciate.

And so we thank the Lady of the Lakes
for taking us on this heavenly break.
A memory now, though we'll never forget
a pity Cumbria's not nearer is our one regret.

The hotel a perfect place to rest and dine,
the staff so smart, so young, but so refined.
All goes well with a glass of smooth white wine.
So we raise our glasses to one and all
Thank You, and You Dear Mary, most of all
'Your very good health.'

*(*Merrow - village near Guildford, Surrey)*

Derek C J Jones

Words

Wherefrom this English that we write?
Left from many a different time;
What perfidy bestowed us this?
Such trouble to pen a simple rhyme.

Is it this, or is it that,
A simple language do we joke?
An easy task to get it right,
Yet must I labour for half the night!

Should language dwell for its own sake,
On words held over 'till they rot?
What life, what meaning should it have?
But allowing us now to convey a thought.

Academics yet will ramble on,
Like braying donkeys in full song;
'Conform! conform!' So tighter tie the noose,
Who dare disturb their golden goose!

But take a simple test to see,
Could ever, two referees agree?
Those who master it, what do they do,
Adjust their foot, to fit the shoe?

Alistair McLean

Just A Chance Meeting

The evening was quiet as I walked through the meadow,
Summer sun sinking and casting its shadow,
Warm, balmy air that would stir a young swain
To kiss his new sweetheart, and undying love claim.

My mind began to wander, as if in a dream,
I felt the overwhelming loneliness of being alone
With no-one to share the peace, and tranquillity, of this beautiful scene
Where rhododendron shrubs were guarding the stream
That flowed in soft ripples from its source on the moor.

I met a fine lady taking the air,
Then, as if to answer an unspoken prayer,
She gave me a smile, which, I declare,
Was of unequalled sweetness, quite beyond compare.
I felt my heart quicken, just miss a beat,
And knew in an instance, that we would meet
Again, somehow, somewhere.

Some days later, we did, by chance, meet again
With the time to spend a most delightful day
Rambling the moor, talking quite freely, sharing our thoughts,
And our hopes for the future, wherever that lay.

We recognised then, the strong sparks between us, igniting emotions
That never could burst, into an all consuming flame,
For our life-paths were set, with other devotions
That had to be honoured or else lead us to shame.

We parted as friends, as perhaps was best,
For we never set out to put ourselves to the test;
Maybe in time, or as our destinations wane
We can meet again, to refire the flame.

Edgar Wall

Coming Home

I have this strange obsession
When I visit my old home,
For when I've kissed my mum and dad
I really have to roam.
I peer round doors to every room
Examine every space,
To see that nothing's altered
All is in its usual place.
The books must be in order,
The ornaments just so,
I even have to look in drawers
To check the status quo.
I know it seems peculiar
This obsession that I have
For constantly ensuring
All's the same with mum and dad,
The reason is quite simple
It's my past I'm checking on,
All my childhood memories
Where my dreams have all sprung from,
The things that made me what I am
That formed my sense of place,
That gave my heart its purpose
Fortified me for the race;
And now that I am settled
With a child all my own,
I often look about me
As I pass from room to room,
I'll try to keep from changing things
Wherever I may roam,
So when my daughter visits me
She'll know that she's come Home.

Caroline Isherwood

Adventures In Pictures

I'm no expertise on 'Mod-art' paintings as such -
Vincent Van Gogh was a brilliant artist - he himself was born
Dutch,
Tho' I'm hardly a qualified critic to enable me to suggest this
much
But according to an article relating to the British born L S Lowry
He was a whimsically unusual character, seemingly serious and
sourly,
Many of his creative sketchings of the widely known 'Matchstick
Men'
Were originally drawn with coloured crayon, pencil and black
pen,
For his works of art, he became a popular figure, and world
famous,
Long recaptured like 'Olivier', 'Shakespeare' and the legendary
'Bette Davis',
Observing the sad. Less fortunate folk as if their deformaties
were an entertaining joke.
Tho in truth, his attentive interest in the malformed and the
lame -
Inspired in him - 'True Life' - bringing to him greater glorified
fame -
For their pictured plights in frame are much admired by us all -
Among his collectors L S Lowry's valued paintings are proudly
exhibited in the arts hall

Eleanor Haydon Sanderson

The Sorrows Of Sarajevo

Auld Man in the moon, you ride high each night
Watching so silently the battles they fight,
Battles of words both silent and loud,
You so alone and they in a crowd

You seem to be looking as if from one eye
We ponder your vision and ask ourselves why
We wonder what thoughts do pass through your mind
You must see a lot yet the answers you find
Are kept to yourself as you look down to say,
Tomorrow is coming, forget the past day

But forget is a word so small in itself
You can't pack or parcel and store on a shelf
Auld Man in the Moon, as you ride there up high
Watch those in sorrow, don't let them cry

For as we pass beneath you and the cripples try to walk
Offer some forgiveness to those that wish to talk
It need not be of ethics, or to whom they pray each day,
Their sorrow is unending, their pain is here to stay

Words perhaps are meaningless, prayers are said instead,
The naked must be covered, the hungry must be fed
Maybe some words of pity will ease a tortured mind
Might take away the heartache, bring peace to a tortured mind
And all the fears and troubles, the endless tears they bring,
Can change to joys and pleasures and the world sing again

E F Croker

London Train

From London town the late night train
Rattles its rhythm through the rain
On the long dark haul to the North

From all walks of life together awhile
A collection of folk ride second class style
On the long dark haul to the North

A 'trendy' with mobile and filofax
Sits near two ladies with bags and macs
They're glad to be heading back North

The city's all right for a spree and a show
But to country places they'd rather go
Not far from their homes in the North

There's a shabby businessman, getting too old
For all this commuting - he's tired and cold
And longs to retire to the North

A mother and daughter have been to town
To buy a designer wedding gown
She'll dazzle them all back up North

A pair of young lovers sit hand in hand
Meeting in secret despite being banned
Escaping at last to the North

Three teenage pop fans no one is keener
Enjoyed a great concert at Wembley Arena
Rock back to the boring old North

My eyes rest upon an old lady sitting
Comfy contentedly patiently knitting
Going home from her son's place where he and his wife
And the kids have all shown her the time of her life

The train slows its pace and pulls into the station
And everyone's eyes seek a friend or relation
To meet them and greet them with welcoming faces
Then bring round the car and help carry the cases

Jennie Dawes

I Fell In Love With Teddy

I fell in love with teddy
When I looked in the shop,
I fell in love with teddy,
And my heart just wouldn't stop.
It beat so fast
But it felt so good,
I knew he'd be mine
I knew he would.
I'd spend hours at the window
In all sorts of weather,
Dreaming of those happy days,
When we would be together.
I'd look into his cuddly eyes
And longed to hold him near,
To have him always by my side
Because I love him dear.
I walked along the street one day
To say hello to Eddy,
But he'd gone from the window
What had happened to teddy?
I cried so much on the way home,
Feeling sad and so alone.
I ran to mum
Who gave me a big hug,
She gave me a drink poured from a jug.
Then she gave me a box sealed with a bow,
I didn't want to know.
So she opened the box,
And what a surprise,
Out popped teddy
In front of my eyes.

I gave him a hug
That lasted forever
So I'm happy now
As at last we're together.

S L Teasdale

A Tribute To Billy

I first met you when I was eight
I knew from then you would be my mate
You were twelve, much older than me
Just very wise - you had to be
You knew all the tricks of the trade
Anything you could do to evade
Billy to me you meant everything
You were my life, friend and king
My grey pony a friend indeed
In the end you were in great need
The vet came to see you in much pain
I knew I would never see you again
But a year on and you're in my mind
I feel your love still as strong and kind
Sandy and Mattie miss you as well
Your best horsy friends you could tell
The day you were taken away from us all
Mattie would whinny for you and call
Unanswered he will remain
Until we all see you again.

Andrea Dummer

Best Is Backwards

My mate Fred is different from the rest,
When he talks backwards for him is best.
It gets quite confusing and it's funny in a way,
For example what he said to me the other day.
'Hello Fred how are you?' I said,
'Dave thanks bad too not' replied my mate Fred.
'Did you go anywhere nice last night with your date Marie,'
'Meal a had and pictures the to went we.'

'What about afterwards' I said 'What did you do then.'
'Club a to us took and up us picked Ben.'
'Picked Ben as well I thought Marie was your date,'
Forgetting he talked backwards he replied 'Daft be don't mate.'

'Sorry Fred mate I totally forgot,'
'Then and now happens it mate worry to not.'
So now you can see how hard it is for me,
Understanding Fred at times can be quite tricky.

'End The'

David Alan Kinch

If

If good wishes grew in the garden
On a great big beautiful tree
I'd pick one and wrap it in paper
With love to you from me

If good fortune was a star in heaven
Then I'd pluck it from the sky
And I'd cover it all in kisses
And the twinkle from my eye

If adoration was measured in kisses
Then you in kisses I'd cover
Because you to me are everything
My girlfriend, my wife, my lover.

Mick Webster

Disaster

Convict escaping over the wall,
Careful 'Mate' you just might fall.
If you fall you could break your back
Or give your head a mighty whack!
Then you'll be thrown in a hospital bed,
Just left to rot until you're dead.
For my 'Friend' you're a waste of space
Just causing grief to all you face.
So think again as you start to climb,
It's safer for you just to do your time!

Kathleen M Andrews

The Skiers

Winter weather cold and bleak
Mountains snow capped white and sleek
Virgin snow until the arrival of people brave
Delighting in the cold they crave
They talk of salomons, wax, and metres
Thirty, forty, fifty
And of footwork neat and nifty
They ride by chair, gondola, or sometimes lift
Upwards full of joy to nature's gift
Thermal cladding, goggles and a pair of skis
Like swallows they descend
Swiftly round each curve and bend
Summer sun and sandy shore
Could not exhilarate them more
Their annual treat of winter snow
Gives their faces a healthy glow
Enjoying winter cold and bleak
On snowy slopes of mountain peak

Hazel Smith

Hullo There . . .

'Hello there, Evie, how are you?
It's nice of you to call.
What's that you say, you have some news
Of Julie, do tell all.'

'She had a baby boy last month!'
Good heavens, I'm struck dumb.
I can't believe it, and the crunch,
Her daughter's only one!'

'Oh, Evie, what a fearful mess,
And her just seventeen.
And what of Michael? . . . I can guess,
He treats her like a queen!'

'But, Ciss, he's only just eighteen,
Too young for them to marry.
He's just a learner in a job
Set up by Uncle Harry.'

'How's Julie coping now she's two
Young babies in her life?
And Julie's father, what's his view
Of his wife's sudden flight?'

'Yes, Julie's mum had now walked out,
Her dad is on his own.
They will divorce; it's come about.
The girl must feel forlorn.'

'My goodness, Evie, what a tale,
It really has upset me.
What can we do? We mustn't fail
To help, and not just pity.'

‘All I can say is, I’m amazed
That this should so have happened.
I would have thought that, through the haze
Of love, they’d used discretion!’

‘Well, there it is, let’s trust that right
Will lend a helping hand.
And that her mum will see the light
And wave a magic wand.’

‘I’ll say goodnight, then, and good luck,
There’s no distress intended.
But come next year, sincerely hope
Her family’s not extended!’

Joyce Ainsworth

Spiral, Spirals, Spiralling

Spiral, spirals, spiralling,
never starting, forever evolving,
never ending, forever dissolving.
Entry isn't easy, the intermediate
is extreme, the exit isn't exact,
the apex is a vortex, the middle is
a muddle, the periphery isn't precise,
the circumference isn't clear, the
diameter isn't distinct and the base
is misplaced.
Spiral round to coil and around to recoil,
trying to confuse, applying to confound,
curling in circles, whirling in cycles,
twirling in arcs, unfurling in folds.
Spirals turn and curve from below and
from above, being difficult to define
upon twisting to entwine.
Spiralling downwards with no edges,
spiralling upwards with no angles,
increasing and ascending to inspire,
decreasing and descending so dire . . .
rotating, repeating, returning . . .
spiral, spirals, spiralling.

Simon King

Lost Childhood

Bright with the sun a young child straying
In the sweet meadow blithely playing
I watched with delight what more entrancing
A child with the breeze and tall grass dancing.
Over the meadow the songbird high winging
Over the pebbles the clear water ringing
Sweet was their music and sweet the child singing
Sweet was the joy to my heart they were bringing.
Bright with the sun no more the child straying
In the sweet meadow no more now playing
I watched with sorrow my heart near to breaking
Dark grew the meadow the sun was forsaking.
Sing songbird over the meadow high winging
Sing clear stream over the pebbles start ringing
I listened in vain and my tears were in keeping
No sound from the meadow but the songbird weeping.

Lily Duncan

A Pain Worse Than Death

I am the fifth of seven sons,
Just three of us remain,
The eldest four have sadly passed away.
And twenty years have come and gone
Yet still I feel the pain
Of seeing father being buried 'neath the clay.

And on each sad occasion,
As the family gathered there,
To see a loved one take his final resting place,
What grieved me more than death itself
Was seeing the despair
And sorrow etched on mother's gentle face.

K White

The Wager

Come forth King of the north
from your vast store of riches
draw and thank the poor that
fought your war.

The King takes from his treasure
a horse to race for his pleasure.
Behind his door he gambles
whilst the poor for their lives
scramble.

The King's sport is horse-racing
no force he's facing only money
he's wasting, not like the poor
alive no more.

The guns are rumbling the kingdom
of the north is crumbling the angel
of the north is tumbling.

The bookmaker steals from all
whom he deals. The rich takes us
to the races their greed covers all
bases, they only miss us when we
are not in our places.
Be a sport pass the port.

Vann Scytere

Rubbish

The dumping age is all the rage,
It is evident far and wide.
Unwanted objects of every age
Little the countryside.
One doesn't go far to see a rusty car
In the woods where the bluebells grow.
Near the river bridge is an outworn fridge
Where the Medway waters flow.
By the Castle moat is a dirty old coat
And trolleys from a superstore.
Next the old oak tree is a broken TV
And old dusty carpets galore.
Garden waste strewn in great haste
Where the roses bloom in the hedge.
A couple of tyres and tangled old wires
Disfigure of roadside edge.
A pair of filthy football boots and two apple tree roots
In the grass where the daffodils lean.
An assortment of cans and some battered black pans
Despoil the spring-like scene.
A bicycle here and some bottles of beer
And plenty of concrete lumps.
Recalling with awe all the rubbish I saw . . .
No wonder that I'm down in the dumps.

Roy Burfield

My Land Of Make-Believe

In my land of make-believe
I sometimes am a mouse
I push my quivering whiskers
Outside my mousehole house,
Into a pot of clotted cream
My trembling nose I douse.
And while my paws I'm licking
A horse I am all kicking,
With shining coat
And tangled mane,
I toss my head as one insane.
Among the hunters chasing fox,
And now I am a Jack-in-the-box,
Up and down for half an hour.
Then I'm a rose in a leafy bower.
Or an Iris blue with stately grace
Beside a web of frosted lace,
And sometimes in a happy mood
I am a nymph in a sunlit wood.
Dancing and prancing in the trees.
Singing a song with the gentle breeze.
I can be a hill, or a grain of sand,
I can be what I like in make-believe land.

Dorothy Beaumont

She Breaks The Waves Of Distress

She breaks the waves of distress,
All with a strong determined mind,
Flashing like opals and diamonds of the night,
The significant vibrations come to rest.

Listening with audacious pride,
Love conquers in the ultimate test,
Where discontentment is finally drowned,
Oh she is a loyal gal, for she is the best,

Silent and combining in stillness of zest,
Let the heaving anchor go to the bottom in rest,
Oh worthy champion e'er and there,
The sweet maiden of Utopia fair.

Where attractive women stand to endure,
Blasting fourth on their triumphant day;
Good ladies of victory's house and way,
Where Venus rises far across the bay.

Not every man has known the protection she commands;
Spurning all adversity across her fertile lands,
Now she breaks the waves of distress;
Oh how great and mighty she is in fortitude's dress.

How each mermaid swims the blue ocean depths;
Forty leagues under the titanic sea,
Where lightning flashes, in continuity, thrashing the lee,
Notwithstanding fools and merrymaker's who might be,

She breaks the waves of distress,
Where mighty trombone's wrestle in sweet harmony,
Singing a vivacious song in her blue midnight dress,
Where God's virtue find all who come to caress.

The many talents that we all possess,
In the event of a persistent will,
Persevering by the School and mill,
Knowledge, that potent force in the professors till,

Rhyming and amusing each student's fill,
Food for thought the phantom's light,
As the great spectre fills your world with sight,
Roaming the world as a good traveller's flight.

She breaks the waves of distress,
All with a strong determined mind,
Flashing like opals and diamonds of the night,
The significant vibrations come to rest.

James S Cameron

Tight Lines

There they stand, trophies held aloft,
Glowing with pride at their achievement.
Astride the grassy bank, as breezes waft
Through willow's dancing fronds.

'Let the line run,' the heroes cry,
'This one's a good 'un, see him writhe
And dive. He's strong! He'll try
To make a fight of it.'

I wonder, have they ever thought
How it must feel to drown in air,
Held firmly by a line stretched taut
Through those once peaceful ponds?

Big, strong gladiators of the 'sport',
Pitting their wits against the sleek
And shiny-scaled, so slippery when caught
And landed on the grit.

I'd like to see Them, dangling high,
Mouths stretched and torn by piercing hook.
So animal-lovers passing by
Could stop and take a look.

Hilary Salisbury

The Cat Knows All About It

Who laps all the lovely fresh cream,
With eyes tight closed, like in a dream.
Who rolls on the daffodils,
Who muddies the windowsills.
The cat knows all about it.

Who leaves dabs of hair everywhere,
Who is it who sleeps on my chair.
Who shuns every tin that is shown,
But who is it whose tummy has grown.
The cat knows all about it.

Who is it knows just the right place,
Who is it puts smiles on my face.
Who is it who must have a lap,
Who likes little birds in a flap.
The cat knows all about it.

Who is it who knows every star,
Who is it sits under the car.
Who is it whose spirit is free,
Who loves to sleep under his tree.
The cat knows all about it.

Who suffers our insular lives,
Who is it who doesn't take wives.
Who drapes on my pillow and grins,
Who is it who always wins.
The cat knows all about it.

Diane Brown

Spooks

Walking up a long dark stair
When suddenly I became aware
A woman standing near a post
I wondered, was she a ghost?
Draped in flowing robes of white
She gave me such an awful fright
And not having any guts at all
I turned and floated through the wall

David Brownley

A Pilgrim's Tale

I strode along a beaten track
in the Cheviot hills one day,
the sky was blue with scattered clouds
and I sang along the way.
The view was great, my pack felt light,
the hills were rolling out of sight.
No other mortal could I see,
it seemed the world belonged to me.
I loved the solitude, the calm,
with nought in sight to do me harm.
My lungs were full of fresh, clean air,
and a cooling breeze ruffled my hair.
Then suddenly the fog came down
and rolled in swathes along the ground.
I couldn't see two feet ahead,
my lonely walk now filled with dread.
My progress it was very slow
as I didn't know which way to go.
I slipped, and fell, and broke my leg
and lay quite still as if I'm dead.
In pain I saw my bleeding limb,
and gave my shattered bone a glance,
I closed my eyes in helplessness
and lay quite still as in a trance.
How long I lay I do not know,
but I awoke to see a glow
as some strange person shook my arm
and stilled my fears with his great charm.
This man, who had a bearded face
seemed quite unreal at this lost place.
His clothing made an old world picture,
like an ancient saint out of the scriptures.
He bent and touched me once again
and I relaxed and felt no pain.
I closed my eyes, then sat up straight,
my helper gone - he did not wait.

I saw the blood on sock and ground
but on my leg no wound was found.
The fog it cleared and I moved on
my pain and injury had now gone.
I saw the blood on sock and ground
but that bearded man I never found.
So what did happen on that day
when I fell down and lost my way?
That blood was on my sock to see,
but I had no wound, which puzzled me.

Walter Christmas

The Reluctant Atheist

(In memory of Francois Mitterand, 'I am a reluctant atheist. If there is a God, I hope he will welcome me nevertheless.')

Encroaching cancer forces me again to ponder
The stark realities surrounding life and death,
The frailties of my body causing me to wonder
If I condemned too easily the claims of faith.
What evidence is there? Can earth's disasters,
Can rampant evil, round, below, above,
Can they encourage me to heed the masters
Who claim the Universe is built on love?
And yet, how can this intricate creation
Just happen, lacking any guiding mind?
Is evil just a passing aberration
Intruding on the goodness God designed?
If all my unbelief should prove to be mistaken
Will God forgive my sin and deign to reawaken?

Vaughan Stone

Spindrift

Long ago and distant, in days gone by,
When ships lay in the anchorage from Winchelsea to Rye,
With the wind in the ratlins, and the salt in the breeze,
And the tavern signs swinging to a song of the seas,

Then the crews'd sing a shanty, or a sad Spanish air,
And the bold freebooters, 'trading' south of Finisterre,
Would come a-dancin' and a-fiddlin' and a quaffin' of the ale,
With a wink and a chuckle, and a far-off tale.

But, while I stand a-dreaming of those days gone by,
The Romneys graze the farmers' fields from Winchelsea to Rye;
For the waterways have silted and the grass blows free,
And the ships have sailed forever, and gone is the sea.

Like a squat and rugged sentinel, the sun-tanned town of Rye
Rises sharp from out the misty marsh, its ancient bulwarks dry;
And like a shrunk old salt a-sleeping awaits Winchelsea the tide:
Their medieval puissance drained, these ports of stranded pride.

Yet, sighing through the sand-dunes when the south winds blow,
There comes a distant echo of a time long ago
That sets my heart a-throbbing, as I harken there -
To a salt sea-shanty, or a sad Spanish air.

Bernard Brown

Ruby Time

Do you remember when the days were long
In strawberry time?
And how the world was wrapped in love,
And life sublime.

In those young years the summers seemed bejewelled
In red rose time.
And crimson suns turned seas to fire
At evening chime.

But now we gather all those memories
At ruby time,
And strawberries, roses, oceans, jewels
Glow red in rhyme.

Mary Daniels

Poultrycide!

(A mock-heroic poem - with apologies to Pope - to commemorate the untimely death of certain cherished domestic fowl)

Of crested roosters taken on the wing,
of feathered bi-peds and of dogs, I sing,
and beg the Muse to guide my moving quill
to tell of houndish evil hated still.

The ducks were mute, the pullets in their nest,
the chickens mothered deep in downy breast;
softer than music when the cadence falls,
so played the wind upon the midnight walls.
Who could have scented in its pleasing breath
the fatal omen of approaching death?

Bounding from darkness to the wall there sprang
a hound with vicious eyes and fearsome fang.
The bark that tore the silence from the trees,
cutting the air, made human blood to freeze.
Before those dove-tailed dreams had been dispelled,
before that poultry peace had been expelled,
there lay a bleeding corpse upon the ground -
it rose, it fell, it died without a sound.

Then chaos reigned supreme as order fled
and none could tell the living from the dead.
A snow of plumage bleached the falling air
and drifts of duck lay bleeding everywhere.
The ducks, the drakes, the hens and cocks as well
all in a moment, unprepared, they fell.
Who would not grieve to look on such a sight?
A wholesale slaughter in a single night.
The deed is done, the mongrels slink away
in fear lest THEY should fall, another's prey.

Mary McKeone

What A Loss

The little children play around
Without a single care
Their happiness and peace of mind
We think of as so rare
Yet we once had that rarity
That little children do
Oh! What a loss oh! What a loss
A loss to me and you
So growing up can change the game
And hide and seeks no more
And castles that were built of sand
Lie dead on the seashore

Abigail Jones

Slimming Days

I've tried so hard to slim
As I dived in the biscuit tin
Rubbish, hubby said
If you don't go to bed
You will look like dusty bin.
So I joined a club called J&M
I met Jane and Susie and Mrs Benn.
Now Mrs Benn had a problem too
She would like to weigh just eight stone two.
She said to me with such a frown
I have a problem bending down.
So with the help of J and M
I agreed to slim with Mrs Benn
She lost three stone and I lost two
It can be done so persevere too.

Elsie Keen

Once More With Feeling

I want to be kissed
And feel that I'm missed

I want to make love
Under Egyptian stars

I want to reach heights
Grasp Venus and Mars

I want to fly above the storm
And be re-born

I want to experience all these things
I am how old nearly . . . I deserve my 'wings'

So . . . once more with feeling
Or am I still dreaming?

Elaine Edgar

Children

Children give us pleasure,
That much I do believe,
We mould them into who they are,
Or what we can achieve.

We try to teach them right from wrong,
By showing them the way,
But they must be given
The chance to have their say.

They must have their own identity,
It will be different from our own,
That's what they are entitled to
No one should be a clone.

We bring them up the best we can,
Instil in them some hope,
But that doesn't guarantee, when
They are older, they can cope.

K P Mundee

The Debt We Owe

Oh yes! I remember Ivan Petrovich Pavlov very well,
I knew him from the past and have much to tell;
They say he made himself quite a name,
And has entered the human hall of fame.

Oh yes! I recall the times with a shiver,
The sound proofed room, the metronome, the buzzer;
The inserted tube in the jaw, the measurement of saliva,
The tantalising wait for food, the pangs of hunger.

Very punctilious and rather eccentric would be our lighter epitaph,
Using strange terms in whispers to his staff;
Excitation, inhibition, conditioned reflexes by technical name,
Equating them all the human frame.

But Pavlov and his dogs were no laughable circus act,
For we did advance the science of psychological fact;
And proud I am to have been involved in this aim,
Showing that canines and humans have much to the same.

It is time for us to claim some of the glory,
So that when you meet us in the country way,
Easy going, docile, and as family pets on the limited lead,
You will raise you hats, and in gratitude concede.

Eric Ashwell

Inner City Illness

Welcome to Hell's prescription
Purpose lost and no direction
Heart of the cosmos gone
Muddled minds what have they done?

Kick a dog when it's down
Kick the sick to the ground
Stamp on the heads of the bowed
Whose in charge in the crowd?
Can't get a name -
Who do you blame?

Empty eyes peer from a shrivelled frame
Shoulders slumped who's to blame?
Sigh leaves the lips-no-job-or health
No nice home or wealth.

Someone somewhere has stolen our dreams
They came one day and sucked them away
Never mind-take a pill, have a jar -
Wipe-out the past,-present-forget how far
You have slipped
On your next trip.

J Dickinson

Riverside

When life is full of trouble or just becomes a bind
The best therapy you could ever have, is with a rod and line
You've chose your bait, cast your line, now it's time to wait
And while your eyes are on that float, gently bobbing there
The mind is free to enjoy, the peace without compare
The steady flowing river, as it meanders on its way
Does it not reflect our lives, in a similar kind of way
You've sat here two hours or more, of that you'll not be sure
For time its self is meaningless, when the river you explore
It's time you should be homeward bound, your trip was not in vain

For the creatures you have seen today
To have missed would be a shame
A water rat and moorhens, the swans and squirrels too
Have all in turn throughout the day, popped out to look at you
Your home at last, had your tea, settled in your chair
You close your eyes, and there it is, that float a bobbing there
And as that float just glides away, you strike, become aware
The only bit you've had all day, is in your favourite chair.

D R Blackwell

Morning Mirth

Armed with strong oaken stick,
Lucky my dog on lead,
Off to fields walking quick,
Glittering sun mist-freed.
In rain lyric lark mounts up high,
All-weather wonders glorify.

Along the bridle path,
Riders spy foxes run,
Down burrows in the heath;
Hark how birds chirp with fun.
Shady spots fresh beauty disclose,
In hedges bloom the pink dog rose.

Beyond the noise of vans,
Charms the silent landscape.
Rich flowering hue spans
Across mead to seascape.
Vistas of beauty long and high,
Hold and thrill every eager eye.

Lucky streaks through thick grass,
Up summits with great skill.
Flash of orchids surpass,
Tall trees which woodland fill.
Lawns, scented flowers, bracing air,
Nature's choice way through anxious care.

So shall our morning walk,
Through groves of oak and pine,
Tune us to hear God talk,
By banks of eglantine.
Daily we gain supporting might,
Gloom vanishes in purest light.

James Leonard Clough

The Clock

The gleaming bob swings slowly to and fro
and beats the fleeting seconds as they go.
The brazen bell the hours doth proclaim,
while fretted hands do indicate the same.

Two hundred years have passed since it was new,
and every second since has measured true.
Unerringly the minutes ticked away,
without a pause by night or through the day.

The phases of the moon were shown aright,
important once to travellers by night.
The highway man and poacher too would know
which nights upon their business they should go.

Each generation knew it as a friend
a witness of their birth and at the end.
Its stately presence comforted their sorrow
with promise of a better day tomorrow.

As through the years the seasons come and go
From balmy summer days to winter snow.
Its lofty countenance though so benign
reminds us of the brevity of time.

Janet Cavill

The Primrose

Fresh-washed, spring cleaned by an April shower,
I looked at the primrose, sweet spring flower
As it nestled in its green mossy bed,
Just showing its delicate yellow head.
I looked at the beauty all around me
Giving such enjoyment, yet all so free.
My heart is grateful for such a treasure;
A God given garden for our pleasure!

Mary Week

Never Satisfied

'Oh, isn't it cold!' I cried everyday
As the east wind blew and the sky was grey.
Roll on summer! - It would be nice
To walk the dog without slipping on ice.
Let's hurry home and make some hot tea
And sit where it's warm and watch TV.

'Oh! Isn't it hot!' I gasped everyday
As the sun waxed hot on the dusty way.
Roll on winter! - I am a fool
To walk the day when I can't keep cool.
Let's stroll home and sit in the shade
With a tall cool glass of iced lemonade.

J Stewart

A Hymn Of Praise And Commitment

Praise to the Lord in all his might,
His radiant face hid from our sight.
He only is the total love
Who sent his son from high above.

In Jesus Christ we know our Lord.
He came to earth to be the Word.
In human form He gave his life
To put an end to hate and strife.

At Pentecost the Spirit came
To set our hearts and souls aflame;
And still He works amongst us all
If we will listen for the call.

As stewards of the holy word
The total truth we must preserve
And pass it on to those to come -
Before we reach our final home.

So praise the Lord, the Three in One,
And pray through us His will be done;
To spread his truth through all the earth:
Nothing can be of greater worth.

E D Sulston

The Hurricane

The cloudless sky was a clear blue
The sparkling sea was so calm too
When suddenly across the bay
Appeared a swirling column of grey
Which sucked salt water from the deep
Then spewed huge waves so rough and steep
Most ships were wrecked and all storm tossed
Whilst many a precious life was lost
Then on it whirled towards the shore
A hundred miles an hour and more.
It swept the beach's golden sand
For several miles across the land,
Trees were uprooted, homesteads fell
And furniture was smashed as well.
The shrieking ceased; not a sound
Except of mourning all around.
All that was left that island fair
Was devastation and despair.

Barbara Saum

Memories

Memories are made of this, tender thoughts of our last kiss,
Having to tear our lips apart
Each knowing the pain in our hearts
In our minds lie empty days
Memories of long gone ways
Those wasted days, years of bygone era
Makes both our needs dearer
The bygone years fled swiftly by
They kept us apart I wonder why
Our memories now have come true
Hoping God grants us years anew
Our love no more shall be memory
What was a memory is now alive
It's up to us to make it thrive
Be always proud to admit
The story of memories shall stay
A lover's hit.

Bertha Shuttleworth

Chasing Time

One morn, the boy saw her,
Just at break of day,
Determined, he chased her
But she flew away
And kept on flying, flying, flying
Before him all the way,
He kept running, running, running
Hands outstretched, clasping, losing
But instead of her golden hair
His hand held only air
                    And he stopped, breathless.

At noon, the sprite became
A golden maiden
And he sprang out
From his lethargy again
But her graceful form
Kept running away, away, away,
Dazzled, exhausted, he retired.

At evening, in his prime, matured,
He started a fresh pursuit
But she, though a rounded matron
Could run quicker than her patron
Through the dance she led him,
                    Faster, faster, faster.

At night, when he was just skin and bone,
He spied the old crone
And despite his age,
His few teeth grinding in rage
He again took up the chase,
But She Won The Race
And he fell down dead.

Mary Frances Mooney

Diana - Our Sorrows For You

The day you died, our Lord was mad,
he turned the blue sky,
grey and sad,
he brought the rain
or were they his tears,
he was not expecting you
for many, many years.

You have left behind you, two young sons
that now have to grow up
without their beloved mum,
our hearts are with them
at this sad time
what happened to you, was such a crime.

You were full of love, and compassion too
you cared so much for the people
and we all cared for you.
You were too young to be taken
I thought the newscaster was mistaken,
now there is anguish, upset and sorrow
all over our great nation.

Children weeping, mother's too
these tears Diana
are all for you,
our nations lost the most perfect rose,
our hearts are sad
and our sorrow grows.

Susan E Senior

A Wash-Out

Three weeks, in a caravan, everyday, in pouring rain,
Coping with a leaking roof, really, was a strain,
The rain, battering, on the roof, awoke us all, at dawn,
And the person, fetching water, had to put, their wellies on.

We played at cards, to pass the time, or sometimes, played a game,
Everynight, praying for sun, but next day, was just the same,
The floods, around the caravan, looked, a terrible mess,
'Cos everyday, we expected to see, the monster, from Loch Ness.

We didn't need, sun-specs, or lotion, but were weather-beaten, no doubt
And we really, saved our money, 'cos we never got out,
Now having, water-meters, was being planned, by some folk,
But a shortage, of water, in Scotland, really, is a joke.

Jean Hendrie

Trees

Humming bees buzzing by,
Say the trees never lie,
So that is why they say they see,
That you don't really care for me.

Do I believe the things they say,
Or do I hope that you'll someday
Remember how we used to be,
And hope that you'll again love me.

The butterflies wings that brush my cheek,
Refuse to hear the words I speak.
They say the same things as the bees,
Just listen to the sturdy trees.

Always they are strong and true,
Never will they lie to you.
Always there to lean upon,
Tomorrow you won't find them gone.

Monica D Buxton

Seasons

Kaleidoscopic horizons deepen and fall,
Autumn is fading transmitting the call
For self-preservation to each of a kind,
Assiduous tasks employing each mind.
Migrating vertebrates gather en masse,
To follow their instincts, ignoring each class.

Wild inspiration reduces and dies,
Hiding beneath darkening skies.
Feathery wisps of white chimney smog
Rise endlessly upwards amassing the fog.
Blizzards and gales sweep landscapes afresh,
Cascading temperatures bite at the flesh.

Christmas arrives with a welcoming zest,
The comforting uplift applauding the rest.
New Year brings forth the emergence of spring,
Reviving alertness, encasing each thing.
Habitats bustle with vigorous spice
As wildlife returns to balance the dice.

Each generation procuring their breed,
Each vegetation implanting its seed.
Warm thermal breezes caress the cool air,
Announcing that summer vocation is here.
Relaxing refreshment takes charge of the mind
For leisure and pleasure to calmly unwind.

Green panorama highlighting the view
Of seasonal sequence dictating the queue,
As solar magnetics induce the firm change
To autumn's familiar and graphical range.
Long evenings shorten and hearing the call,
Kaleidoscopic horizons deepen and fall.

Josephine Duthie

Night

Why does night descend so fast?
Now that summer days are past
Evening shadows heavy fall
Darkening and engulfing all.

Relentless to the lonely one
Who longs for the summer sun
Days of fog and winter chill
Make the night a bitter pill

When after darkness comes the dawn
And at last it is the morn
Appears a brilliant ray of light
To banish the unending night.

As the night descends again
Causing the forsaken pain
Time hangs heavy like a sign
Dragging down the stars that shine.

Pamela Joyce

Wild Flowers

Look yonder into the hedgerow
Look ye back into the past
Primrose, bluebells long since gone
          Alas eternal beauty does not last

In the eyes of mass humanity
Weeds are remembered by the few
Flowers like the primrose of springtime
          Become solace in the morning dew

Babes once played in yonder fields
No time for thoughts of fear nor fright
Gone sweet daisy wort and dandelion
          Like passing strangers in the night

Where foxglove once stood tall and proud
Vine now spreads midst moss and grass
Flowers extinct, dead and dying
          Seen only now by schooltime class

Wild flowers once grew in woods and fen
And I had seen them all
Etched deep within my memory
          When I was very small

The future now like a rambling rose
Holds onto the crumbling past
Sweet flowers now long since gone
          Alas, eternal beauty does not last.

Jeanne E Quinn

Once Upon A Time

A sea danced
and frolicked with delight.
And sea horses pranced and
rode the waves, frothy and white.
That was of course before
man took waters from its resting place and
now has bigger problems to face.
Fishing villages desolate, hearts full of hate.
All the men folk gone, no laughter or song.
Salt burns the eye, passes nothing by.
Never is heard the call of the sea bird.
It makes one feel sad and more than mad.
To think the sea God created was in this way fated.
God created the sea to flow and be free.
Not be tampered by man, that wasn't God's plan.
Man has surely sinned, salt blown in the wind.
He has spoiled and defaced and left an eerie
empty space.
Boats marooned high and dry. Man forced a living
sea to die.
Leaving a residue of salt, this again is man's fault.
For irrigation the sea was drained, until not a drop
of water remained.
Only a sickening, sad and sorrowful sight.
The sea God created with all His power and might.
Never again, will the waves wash the shore and glisten
in the moonlight.
We must wholeheartedly, sympathise with the fisherman's
plight.

Elizabeth Myra Crellin

Could This Be Love?

What is this I'm learning?
When my stomach starts a churning
when he walks into a room
and my heart begins to boom.

How come I feel so weak,
when I see him in the street,
then he smiles and says 'hello'
and my face begins to glow.

My eyelids start to flutter,
and all I can do is stutter,
where have all my words gone?
As I stare and bite my tongue.

What is this I'm feeling?
When my head starts a reeling,
when my legs begin to shake,
then my heart begins to race.

Could this be my heart he's stealing?
Are these butterflies I'm feeling?
Is this my heart that tugs?
Could this really be love?

Kathleen Tutty

Thank You

you gave me love
you gave me happiness
you gave me strength
you gave me pleasure
what we have will last forever
which no one can ever take away
what we have is here to stay
it will never ever go away

Daisy Helen Thompson

My Imaginary Place

The cobbled walls,
The bright green trees.
The beautiful buildings,
The afternoon breeze.
A place where I spend my melancholy days.
One beautiful place I can watch the cows graze.
I hear the music of birds wings flapping,
The soft humming rhythm of the water lapping.
The exquisite tall arch of the cathedral,
The lazy droning noise of chattering people.
Golden bells in the tower ring, ding ding ding.
The anchor splashing in the deep blue river,
The glowing white seagull hovering hither.
The clouds drifting slowly above,
The bright red roses remind me of love.
Just to suit my kind of taste,
Yes, my imaginary place.

Derica Shields (11)

Night Moves

As I lay on my bed at night,
I sense deep inside, that all is not quite right.
The delicate tinkle of a sweet kitten's bell
Silhouettes of foxes in the dell.

I gaze from my window into the black velvet of night
Knowing all creatures are busy acknowledging their right!
They burrow and visit and pay their respects
And on their way, they consume insects.

The hedgehog ambles in his nonchalant manner
Pretending all night that he's Lord of the Manor!
The spider climbs the drainpipe for the umpteenth time
Hoping to find unsuspecting prey to entwine.

In his silvery web, so strong and so fine
Making filigree patterns, that are so divine.
My attention is taken by the hoot of an owl,
But then still the old tom cat is out on the prowl.

As the silvery moon highlights the sky
Was that a fruitbat I saw passing by?
I gaze at the clock as I stifle a yawn
I really must sleep some, before the new dawn.

Avril Ruby

Red Snow

What would happen if we had red snow
Would the countryside brightly glow,
We could have red snowball fights
They would glow like red fluorescent lights,
But what would happen when darkness fell
To be out in red snow would be sheer hell,
The little robin would get such a fright
He'd have to change his breast from red to white,
The berries on the holly tree
Would have to change quite drastically,
What would happen if we had red snow
Rudolph's nose would no longer glow,
Father Christmas could no longer dress in
His long red flowing robe
What a headache that would be for he's so
Well known around the globe.
What would happen if we had red snow
Would pantomime have to go,
Sure Snow Red and the Seven Dwarfs
Wouldn't be the same kind of show
Those are some things that might happen
If we had red snow.

C J Black

Not So Great For Some

Men suffered the horror's of the trenches,
Women making munition's sat on benches,
The Great War an event that broke down fences,
Fashion's evolved to enhance a man's fancies,
On the dancefloor we began to see new dances.

It was remarkable some survived those trenches,
Battered and bruised they protected the countries defences,
Some still shell shocked suffered the pain of a strangers glances,
In the mind memory of the terror and fear often prances,
Hopes for a world of peace what were the chances.

Ann Woolven

Rhyme To Time

It is rhyme to time yes
And time to rhyme
In which all the words must be kept in line
And gently show a sign.

It is rhyme to time tonight
So the kids will sleep all night
Without ever catching fright
Which means they sleep well out of my sight.

It is rhyme to time just before I go to sleep
For a chapter my night time book I am engrossed so deep
But at certain parts I start to weep
Yet at other parts I feel the heat.

Keith L Powell

Joyness Of Love

J is for being joyful and happy,
O is for the order of life,
Y is for having youthful things,
F is to have fun to the full,
U is for us to use life joyfully,
L is to live the life we have known,
L is the love of life you have,

A is for the anger people have,
N is for knowing the newness of love
D is for the dawning of joy,

I is for the inner strength we have,
N is for the newness of joy,

L is for loving your elders and everyone,
O is for owning joy in your heart,
V is having vigour and value in love,
E is for endeavouring to have joy in love.

Sharon Joy Wandless

Goodbye

Tessa Kate Lowe
I miss you so
Not a word
Have I heard
Since Christmas
Alas
It's a mystery
To me
Why this should be
Or how it has come to pass

About fifteen years ago
From Durban you came
To make your name
And find fortune and fame
With two daughters in tow
That is about all I know
Except you've been married twice
And that must suffice
Now I must let you go
So goodbye farewell
I'll withdraw into my shell
Cheerio

W B McDade

Remembering Yew

We go back along way
of past times in history
I recall so many events
holding scenes of mystery

Standing strong, branching out
I see both day and night
nothing is hidden from me
all before my eyes in sight

Yew have lingered by my side
in despairing, confusing thought
I have listened to yew my love
as yew weep in silence alot

I call out to yew, to lay by my side
to heal yewr wounds. I pray
sending to yew all my love
each moment of each day

Consider what yew do to me
showing me such torture
chopping away at my existence
so cruel, sad, sapping murder

Yew may refuse to hear my cries
or turn away when bleeding
I am real life with stemming roots
and branches stretch as sleeping

I stand before yew here today
are yew listening to my call
be an angel once again
Guard against the final fall

Come and sit down by my side
let me nurture all yewr pain
I want to reach into yewr heart
and bring sunshine out of rain

Hope is at the root of me
it can be for yew too
open up yewr trust, my love
remove the fear inside of yew

Do not starve yewrself like this
so hungry and in need
love is what yewr craving for
my offering is the seed

Let's end man's earth destruction
this planet must survive
nurture every living thing
and keep the trees alive

The rain preserves the forest
and for a very good reason
falling down to quench the thirst
to make it through each season

Megan Muran Hunter

The Stick Insect

My daughter came home from school today, clutching a small glass jar
I looked at it suspiciously, you know what children are.
'What have you got there?' I cried 'Oh, whatever is it?'
'It's a stick insect' she said with glee, on a piece of privet
I gazed into the jar, but all that I could see
Was a weary piece of privet that had fallen off a tree.
But as I looked upon a leaf I saw a piece of stick
It wasn't very long and it wasn't very thick
But on that stick there were two eyes gazing back at me
'Take that nasty thing away' I screamed from on the table
'Oh don't be silly mum,' she said 'I'm going to call it Mabel'
'Well she goes or I go' I said, swinging from the lamp.
Me legs had gone all wobbly and my forehead felt quite damp
I don't mind furry spiders, a few mice, even a cat
But a stick with eyes and legs on I couldn't stand for that
So now it's in the garden with a great big hedge of privet
And if she doesn't shut her trap, she'll be out there with it.

Sylvia Derbyshire

How Far To Cambridge? (London To Cambridge Bike Ride)

A July Sunday Bike Ride over hills and flat.
Fifty-eight miles, they say, but just how far is that?

Major roads, dual carriageways, single winding tracks.
Suburbia and hamlets, London at our backs.

Reservoirs and winding streams; factories and shops;
Grazing sheep and barley fields; market-garden crops.

Wild flowers in the hedgerows; blood-red poppy fields;
Combine harvesters progress, collecting their yields.

Splattered hedgehogs and rabbits; woodpigeon and hare
Mark the passages of cars, far too fast to care.

Polite and caring cyclists and gits two-abreast,
Cutting up, weaving through; a nuisance to the rest.

Village halls with home-made cakes; bike checks there on site.
The Red Cross in attendance putting ills to right.

The single-legged cyclist; the bikes dressed up as ducks;
The 'Boxwood Bumsore Bikers' avoiding the rucks.

People waving as we pass; good wishes given.
Sped on our way by sunshine; by tail-winds driven.

And at the end:- fresh doughnuts; coffee and some jazz.
Just dismounting surpasses all razzamatazz!

Mary E Upson

Delight

A blaze of coloured clouds, illuminated by the setting sun,
The glistening sea and landscape, enchant the scenic run.
Flowers and greenery add their beauty,
The orange and lemon groves look so fruity.
A wave from people by a cottage door,
A gesture of pleasure, could we ask for more?
Children tiring from a day of play,
Now to dreams to recharge for another day.
As the distant islands become silhouetted by the glow of the sun,
We relax with friends, for a few drinks and some fun.
If today has been all the rage,
Tomorrow will write another page!

Bill Cross

Running

Run, run, running on,
Pacing out the miles,
Run, run, running on,
Footpaths, roads and styles.

Run, run, running on,
Having my own space,
Run, run, running on,
Stepping up the pace.

Run, run, running on,
Sweat upon my brow,
Run, run, running on,
Stress retreating now.

Run, run, running on,
Limits seem to fall,
Run, run, running on,
Freedom is the call.

Run, run, running on,
Spirit soaring free,
Run, run, running on,
At one with what is me.

N D Ifould

Farewell

I would sit and weep, my heart could break
With sense of loss and pain and grief.
He was just an old dog, he was just an old friend
He was just a companion beyond belief.
There's no remorse to shrink the soul,
We loved and cared, we need no crutch
To give support at this sad time.
We just didn't know that we cared so much.
Such warmth, unstinting faith and trust.
We loved our small, dear, canine friend
But we learn that devotion must pay a price
To be balanced by sorrow at the end.
We're resigned, he's gone, his spirit free.
We grieve but we no longer weep.
He was old and tired, his race was run.
Now peaceful, at rest in his long, long, sleep.
But he's there in the magic mind's-eye view,
We can keep him close for all time it seems
For when memories flash back through the years
He returns on the retina of our dreams.

E W Mills

An Ode To Henry VIII

Oh Henry, Henry, you had six wives,
you managed a son and two daughters.
You messed up quite a few people's lives,
and you did a lot better than you ought to.

Poor Catherine who you bullied, how you hurt her,
then you gave her a living so mean, what a sin,
and all for your own so selfish pleasure,
so you could marry that wench Anne Boleyn.
Such a pity it was that she wronged you,
and after all that trouble as well.
You thought finding her was such a coup,
yet who could really know, who could tell?
You managed to get yourself free, with a fight,
and just to be sure, she was beheaded.
You had dallied with sweet Jane, full of light,
then very soon after you were wedded.
Such a lovely girl, she made you so gay,
you no longer were nasty and wild.
It was such a pity sweet Jane could not stay,
but at least she gave you a child.
Poor Henry, how you missed her, you were sad,
yet your newborn son was a wonder.
All wondered if ever again you would be glad,
or if your temper would rise up like thunder.
Your little boy, so young, he was not strong,
most people they feared for his life.
They thought he may not live very long,
and wanted you to choose a new wife.
You fancied a pretty and young lively wench,
One with whom you could have some fun.
someone who your sense of adventure could quench,
a lass whose fair heart could be won.
Your staff had other ideas for your future,
such a plot, your right hand man, he weaves.
He found you a new wife, a Royal suitor,

they brought the unwilling Anne of Cleves.
If ever such a mismatch was made,
this was it without very much doubt.
For this strong minded wench would not be bade,
she very soon made you swear and shout.
You fought quite a while before she went,
she knew you had a fancy for another.
Away from your court she then was sent,
so you could enjoy your new lover.
Fresh young Katherine, so innocent,
Oh Henry, she made you feel so free.
On having her you were so well meant,
yet her youth would age you, if you could but see.
So when she was gone and you felt old,
your ministers they found you another.
One who would make you do as you were told,
a woman who would be like a mother.

Your final years, in comfort at least,
spent with someone so kind and serene.
A widow to care, and tame the wild beast,
she was the sixth, and last, the final Katherine.

Kim McIntosh

Sandown Park

Chastising sun and gentle breeze
Both conspire to unlock, unfreeze
The muscles of the favourite mare
Emerging from her horsebox care.

'Last chance today,' her trainer said
Before he put her down to bed.
'A win, old girl would ensure that you
Turn out to grass, not into glue!'

His smiling eyes and chuckling face
Cajoled her from the deep disgrace
That seven 'ducks' from seven starts
Had not won over punter's hearts.

The jockey kissed her on the cheek
With whispered love; a gentle tweak,
He mounted her with practised grace,
Heart-hoping she would win this race.

The paddock sleuths were out in force.
Eyeing the aspects of each horse
That paraded the racing game
Of losing, winning, fear and fame.

Into the stalls; a silence fell
Upon the crowd. Furlongs of hell
Stretched out to tame yet amuse
A sea of faces; blinkered views.

Starter pulls! Battle commences!
Distance too short for hurdles, fences.
Just sprinting through wet turf and pain
Our lady wins. All hearts to gain.

Cheers from the course erupt at this;
A victory culled from a kiss
T'wixt man and horse. His lady fair
Coaxed back into a life of care.

M Stacey

Goodbye Riverbourne Road

Goodbye Riverbourne Road
You have witnessed fifteen years of my life
Heartbroken widow, aunt, grandma, happy wife
With my thoughts and furniture stowed.

Goodbye Riverbourne Road
Thank you for protection against wind and weather
The occasional flash of a kingfisher's feather
A welcoming warm abode

Goodbye Riverbourne Road
You have withstood all the changes well
Double glazing, decoration and a conservatory to swell
Your contents which pride can't erode

Goodbye Riverbourne Road
I shall miss the peaceful riverbank beauty
Midst primroses, leafy trees, duck feeding's not a duty!
By the elements you're never bowed

Goodbye Riverbourne Road
You will soon be a vast empty shell
My belongings withdrawn-future happiness-who can tell?
Fear and hope go along with the load.

Goodbye Riverbourne Road
I must leave whilst the tears keep at bay
Thanks for being my home, I just cannot stay
As seeds of a brighter future are sowed!

Gillian Blake

Why

Why is the balance of nature?
Not balanced so very well.
Why do some live such an easy life?
Yet others endure sheer hell.
Why do the humble ask for very little?
Taking only what they need,
Whilst many reach for everything
But cannot fulfil their greed.

Why so many childless couples?
Although orphanages overflow.
Why are minefields left un-defused?
Where innocent victims go.
Why exhaust entire plantations?
Of natural trees and shrubs.
Why leave top-soil vulnerable?
To wind and rain and floods.

Why can't humans ever learn?
From all their past mistakes.
If planet earth is to carry on
We've got to give and take.
Why not put all our expertise?
Into peace instead of war.
Why not leave all other species?
To do the job they are designated for.

Why not try to live in harmony?
What an achievement this would be.
Why not cut back on all pollution?
On land in the air and sea.
Why not put all these dreams into action?
Make our world a much kinder place,
Then perhaps there's a chance of survival
And a future for the Human Race.

Marion Dargue

Brigade Bride

Line side,
Fire time,
Burn up,
Hose down,
Rung, round,
Stretchered fume.
Helmet yellow,
Sharpened axe,
Brass slide,
Bunk duty,
Bar leaning,
Engine gleaming,
Emergency night,
Brigade bride.

J Canty

Untimely

Two days before that Paris crash
(I'm sure you'll know the one I mean)
I'd written a poem on Di and Dodi
Which now of course will never be seen

The days before had been
Frantic with conjecture
Di could rejoice
With ecstatic freedom
Of ultimate choice
A new yacht to explore
A new man to adore
The future was bright,
It held back the night.

Now, only the memory
Of all those flowers remain
And lingering with their perfume
On the air we hear the haunting refrain
Of 'A candle in the wind dying
Again, and again and again.'

Bryn Bartlett

The Firmament

Ever changing never still
Passing over dale and hill
View its pattern while you may
As soon it will have moved away

Cumulus clouds so fluffy white
Bring imaginary pictures into sight
Could it be a wolf or perhaps a bear
Or a lion leaping from its lair

Sometimes above is clear and blue
With dazzling sunshine pouring through
Other times all looks so grey
There seems so little to cheer the way

An occasional thing may cause the eye
To stop and gaze up in the sky
A rainbow formed with colours fair
Reminding of God's love and care

Dawn's horizon when streaked with red
Is thought to denote there are storms ahead
At dusk if it glows in a similar way
May herald the morrow a lovely day

Strung out there are the moon and stars
Even planets like Jupiter and Mars
Such wonderful handiwork everywhere
Created by God for us all to share

Joan Riches

Convenience Commodious

A man called Septimus Arkwright lives in the cottage next door
With his wife Isadora Edwina and a son named Tom
Theodore.
A daughter called Elspeth Amanda lives on the canal in a
barge
With a man known as Franklin Lysander and a guard dog
excessively large.
Aunt Hyacinth comes every Sunday with a cake she has made
for tea;
On best china plates they eat crumpets with a napkin spread out
on their knee.
Mr Arkwright goes off to the city in black bowler, blue suit and
umbrella,
He leaves home every morning at seven after feeding the cat
Isabella.
I'm not sure what he does for a living, it's something important
and serious;
Public service is what he admits too but beyond that it is rather
mysterious.
A young lad by the name of Arbuthnot thinks he's seen
Arkwright's place of employment,
Whilst off to an organised rave-up anticipating abundant
enjoyment,
He went into a subway convenience, a place he'd not used much
before;
It was peaceful and very relaxing with an intricate tiled mosaic
floor.
It was furnished in brown and grey marble, with elaborate
mirrors, gilt-framed
Above gleaming white porcelain wash-bowls and receptacles
all clearly named.
Fluted tulips on bottle green tiling gave the place its Victorian air,
Brass spittoons on the floor in the corners, strategically placed
near a chair.
Highly polished mahogany woodwork gave a luxurious look to
the place,

With panels of heavy plate glasswork creating a feeling of space.
The whole place had a masculine ambience with a library
reading-room hush
And a carbolic wax-polishy smell disturbed now and then by a
flush!
Behind the glass panels sat Arkwright relaxed in a leather
armchair
With a rounded occasional table, pot of tea and a chocolate
éclair.
So, there was nothing really mysterious about Arkwright's job
after all,
But it most certainly was very serious to all gentlemen paying a
call!

Ray Butt

A Stroll In Spring

Today I saw a wondrous sight
A leafless tree lit by sunlight,
'Twas as though it were made of gold
When the sun moved, it looked quite old.

The sunshine then danced on trees of green
A prettier sight I've rarely seen,
And as the sunshine moved again
The trees turned dark and looked quite plain.

A song thrush sang from its perch on high
Its song echoing through a clear blue sky,
The song sounded so melodious
And made this life less onorous.

The rape seed crop was tall and yellow
The fragrance anything but mellow,
Oh what a joy to walk in spring
So pleasant enough to make one sing.

Spring gives me strength to carry on
Along life's great marathon,
The sound, the smells, the joy, the laughter
A life of peace that's all one's after.

Dave Fox

Our Day Out

Mother took the children home
so that next day we could roam.
We started off at the crack of dawn
faces gleaming, hair all shorn.
Driving through the hills and vales,
remembering well old sailor's tales.

Hubby had a tender moment,
as we sailed across the Solent,
put his hand upon my knee and said,
remember darling how it was when first we wed.

We sailed across the sprawling sea,
to where our waiting friends would be,
tying our boat up to the jetty,
we went to lunch with Tom and Hetty

After lots of jokes and talk,
back to the jetty we had to walk.
We supped on ale, and sang a song,
bye dear friends, we'll be back before long.
Happy was the day that ended,
as home our weary way we wended.

Kathleen Collins

The Night Of The Flood

The wind was howling through the keyhole the sea was roaring too
Sitting by the fireside listening to the radio what else could we do
A neighbour brought some sandbags to put against the door
He said there's danger of flooding so I went and got some more

The waves were high and mighty the sandhills it was pounding
And when the gaps appeared the sea then came pouring
A wall of water came sweeping out the gloom
Some people never made the safety of their home

We took some valuables upstairs and only just in time
Water came rushing in bringing in dirt and grime
Then all lights went out we thought our end was nigh
To add to our troubles the water was now five feet high

We sat there cold and hungry with nothing we could do
We huddle together in the dark thank goodness I had Sue
Sitting through this nightmare is sending us round the bend
At last the dawn oh no will our misery never end

Some buildings had collapsed deep water everywhere
No food or drinking water it really is too much to bear
All hope gone now a watery end I fear
No not yet dear look the army is here

Harry Skinn

There's A Hole In My Colander

I sought enlightenment from every age
And then at last I found a Chinese sage
Who shared with me his secret in a trice
'Be certain that you always rinse your rice'.

Stodgy rice, when taken from the pan
Affronts the taste buds of a hungry man
And fail it will, however hard it try,
To complement a succulent stir-fry.

A man whose rice is served without a rinse,
And he, by chance, a potentate or prince,
Will leave the table with his humour raw
And more than likely go and start a war.

But if his rice be (happy potentate!))
Fluffy and dry and each grain separate
His mind will be at peace and so will he
And pleased enough to eat what's left for tea.

So rinse your rice, though effort you need spend,
Thereon the fate of nations may depend.

Lem Ibbotson

Silent Prayer

Quietly I stop talking; I stop working
Peacefully I listen to my heart beating
My thoughts all of a muddle need sorting out
My mind so busy; not always devout

Listen to the sparrows singing in the trees
Watch the insects flying, see the honey bees
Feel the breezes blowing, rustling the leaves
Can I stop for just a second, praying, 'Help me please'

Suddenly my eyes close tight in the middle of the day
This is not the way to pray; this is not my way
No my child it is not; this is My way the Saviour said
As He poured countless blessings on my head

Fiona Higgins

Thoughts In Season

When the wind cries in the night it stops me from sleeping,
It's frightening, as if I'm not in God's keeping.
Raindrops on the window is a comforting sound,
Hurry up you people who are homeward bound.
Winter nights are dark and cold,
Soon it's spring and life unfolds.
Warmth and colour everywhere,
New life, new meaning, from despair.
We must move forward and be bold,
Life and living is still untold.
Summer is coming, everything is blooming,
Now there's no time for sitting and glooming.
The colours in flowers are the colours of life,
Sometimes dim but mostly bright.
Joy and pleasure, more memories to treasure.
A beautiful sky unbelievably blue,
A crowning glory to add to this hue.
Autumn is here before we know it,
Are our minds as mixed as the leaves that show it?
Look at the trees that go on reaching,
Remember only, the thoughts worth keeping.
Life always gives something back from what it's taken,
We must believe that and not be shaken.
Empty our minds, sometimes with a sigh,
One certainly knows a new day is nigh.
Answers are not in the stars.
The stars are in our eyes,
Sometimes truth, sometimes lies,
Life is a game we go on playing,
Follow the path, only the mind goes straying.

Marion P Cook

The Skylark

In a meadow filled with daisies, I
Watched a skylark heavenward fly.
From the green grass, pearled with dew
Up and up to the misty blue.

Small her wing, and sweet her song,
A little brown speck, then lo,she had gone,
I stood and gazed with wondering eye
Will you come back skylark by and by?

Where have you gone? And what will you see?
Oh! Skylark tell the tale to me.
Kissed by the sunshine, midst daisies and dew
I'll sit and wait, and listen for you.

Is it the sheer freedom, up there in the blue,
That makes you sing for joy as you do.
Or is there a land we have never yet seen?
Oh! Tell me skylark, where have you been?

Bertha Dale

Whither Thou Blowest

In the hush of the night
a gentle wind blows
whither thou goest
nobody knows
it flies over hills
and creeps over dales
if it could speak
then what tales
would it tell?

It's been blowing
since life on earth began
witnessed the day
of the birth of man
blew throu' the ages
from years BC to AD
does it whisper of things
that it must see
while it travels?

It has travelled on land
and travelled on sea
but what could it say
to you and to me
it has witnessed the wars
and the follies of man
but with all of its knowledge
does it know of a plan
to save us?

Elaine Setohy

Memories Of June 1998

Summer is here with us once more
Which can only mean sport galore.
Ascot is over once again -
Gorgeous new outfits, same old rain!
Fear not, more cricket's on the way.
Can we keep South Africa at bay?
England hoped for World Cup glory,
Sadly it's the same old story -
Argentina still our bane,
Though not the 'Hand of God' again!
Brave attempts by Shearer, Scholes,
Owen's talent ensured us goals.
But we just missed our victory -
Bad luck, some blame the referee!
Still, England need not cry just yet.
Henman has gone through in straight sets.
It is of Wimbledon I speak
And, as we end the second week,
A Brit in the semi-final,
But to beat Sampras is a tall
Order. I'll end this sporting rhyme,
Save the result 'til the next time.
Finish on a hopeful note here -
Enough sport for another year!

Katherine Dean

They Ran To Save Their Bacon

The nations hearts were really touched, in nineteen ninety eight,
by a story of two little pigs, Butch Cassidy and Sundance his mate,
both of them sentenced to death, and time was fast running out,
so they did what all little pigs do, started digging with their snout.

They tunnelled their way out of the pen, now both were on the run,
from the RSPCA team, who had their lasso's nets and stun gun,
Butch and Sundance became big stars, on everyone's TV screen,
as they eluded the chasing posse, made at times to look rather green.

The chase went on for a two whole days, and still they were not taken,
these two little pigs of great renown, had to run to save their bacon,
eventually Butch and Sundance were caught, both looking very scared,
but thanks to a national newspaper, those two little pigs were spared.

'Twas because they had the will to live, they are alive and well today,
being cared for on a friendly farm, with plenty of mud in which to play,
children go to visit them, they give 'Tit Bits' to Butch and his mate,
and both are very happy, to be saved from someone's dinner plate.

Wenn-The-Penn

Summer Retreat

Summer green leaves
Turning brown
Twisting tumbling
To the ground
Trees stripped bare
Not a leaf to spare
Seeds buried deep
Waiting for spring
To bring some heat
For next summer
Time to reap
Summers hatchlings
Long since flown
Long dark nights
Gale winds blowing
Knitted stripy scarves
Woolly hats and mittens
Young children laugh
Building snowmen
Christmas gifts
Puppies and kittens
Summer times retreat
Now winter has its fete

Ruth Watts

Annie

On the mantel's a cup
for the hundred yard dash
that she won long ago
at the town centre baths.

There's 'A present from Blackpool'
and a card from their Maud
on one of the visits
she once made abroad.

Annie doesn't get out now
except to the shops
plagued by the kids
running wild on her block.

She uses a stick
to keep herself going
and hopes that her fear's
not too obviously showing.

There's a chair that lies broken
and won't be repaired,
a demand from the 'leccy'
that must be deferred.

It seems everyday
there's another fresh bill,
another assault
on her budgetr'y skill.

Four years ago
her Eddie passed on,
so she now keeps his love
in her heart where it's warm.

Nobody visits,
they're mostly all gone,
and there's only reflection
as she looks back alone,
just another old woman
exiled at home.

Jim Rogerson

Trusty Feet

The pavement of life they walk everyday
Knowing not why they go on their way.

Slow and purposeful when we are sad
Fast and skipping when we are glad.

Unclad they tread the soft green grass
To face beneath them, the earth's beating pulse.

Walking in fields, over hills and dales.
Through woods, rivers and mountain trails.

Never ceasing in their quest
To reach a point where they can rest.

On and on daily, they tread
On a cushion of air, or feeling like lead.

Always striving one before the other
To propel our bodies one place to another.

Stop they will, when the time has come
For us to leave our earthly home.

For years they worked to their very best
Now is the time for our feet to rest.

Maureen Gard

A Weekend In Dublin

As we scrambled from the aircraft,
Luggage on our minds.
We waited oh so patiently, so many different kinds,
Looking around for the right exit,
Not an easy task,
Then finding it by accident, just as we're about to ask.

A silver taxi pulls up, and out the driver jumps
Yes, sure I'll take you to Dublin, as in the cases he humps.

He drives as only the Irish can,
Exciting and thrilling for such a little man.
Keeping up the banter in Southern Irish brogue.
It seems he has a family, not really such a rogue.

The Grafton Plaza comes into view
We look at it - something quite new.
Our room is 515 we're told.
We're glad of the lift, as I'm growing old.
Once settled in and postcards written
It's off for adventure, and no more sitting.

The gaiety theatre is two minutes away
We book for the balcony, it's 8pm Saturday.

A ride in a horse carriage in traffic thick
It's a shame for the poor horse,
But just what I'd pick,
To see the Liffy shimmering bright, as
The sun casts its rays catching the light.

Next day we visit the parks and seaside,
The weather is fierce, we take a taxi
And bus ride.
By midday the sun shines again,
We walk through the parks missing the rain.

Shopping was a special treat,
We found clothes half price
And shoes for our feet.
Then out of punts, it's time to go home
We say goodbye to Dublin a friendly
Home from home.

Rosemary C Whatling

It Hurts

So many charities, so many chances to give,
Yet still so many people, needing hand outs to live.
Perhaps we are all guilty of giving, and having too much fun,
Then praising each other, for the good we have done.

Yet, the surfaces of poverty and hunger will be barely scratched,
Until the pain of suffering, and the sacrifice of giving, are evenly
matched.

T J Dean

Sonnet For A Mother

Queen Mother when she left her Scottish land
To give her heart to York, beloved Duke,
Little did think how she would have to stand
When those more senior sacred cause forsook.
All through the war supporting George our King
No shelter did they seek on foreign soil.
So let us of their courage loudly sing
They shared our blood and sacrifice and toil.
Long left alone - her daughter now our Queen -
This Mother has her country's love and knows
We share her memories thus to keep them green
No matter how her mounting years dispose.
God Bless You, Ma'am! And from all ills do save
As we salute the service that you gave.

Denis P J Smith

Mysteries Of London

In Bloomsbury, an Egyptologist
Staggers back in shocked dismay
Before a gilded mummy-case
With open lid, its horrid contents
Spirited away.
Swathed in rotting bandages,
The Mummy drags its way
Down cobbled alleys near the Docks,
Through mist and puddles. Gaunt cats squeal
And bristle at its shuffling feet:
The bleary gas-lamps half reveal
The face that Death had tried to eat.
Far from its sacred tomb,
What does it seek - or whom?

The silver edge of a surgical knife
Is the only visible sign
Of Jack the Ripper, taker of life,
As he lurks by the railway line,
In the shadow of echoing arches
Of slimy brick, which shine
With the trickle of running moisture.
The time is half-past nine.
A policeman's bull's eye lantern gleams.
Jack waits. A clanking goods train steams
Above his head; and now he greets
Another lady of the streets.

Edward Francis

The Slow Fire Lasts Long (A Triolet)

Remember, the slow fire glows and it lasts long.
The fast fire blasts and soon is gone.
Don't be deceived by what might seem strong.
The fast fire blasts and soon is gone.
The same is true of the fiery tongue.
You should pay no heed such a one.
Remember, the slow fire glows and it lasts long
The fast fire blasts and soon is gone.

R L Cooper

Daffodil Wood

I came to seek a sign of Spring,
To reflect, breathe deeply in,
I found a wild forgotten thing,
Egg-yolked, golden, sunrise-bright,
To my eye a sheer delight.

Carpeting the green beneath the trees,
Stretching as far as the eye can see,
Waving softly in the breeze,
Listen to the whispering of the wind,
Listen carefully, Spring begins.

Rachel Gallehawk

Her Man

She sits on the bank listening to her man
As he stands talking, to someone in a van.
Her brown eyes never leaving his face,
She sits quietly, knowing her place.
He raises his hand before stepping back.
Bending down, he picks up an old sack.
Goes to the land rover, opening the door,
And she's on her feet, and ready to go.
Up the hill, fetching sheep from the top,
Working all day 'till they're fit to drop.
They bring down the ewes to the old walled pen
For morning, and the shearing men.
Standing by his side surveying their land
She moves nearer, and touches his hand,
He smiles at her as they move away.
For her, and her man, it's been a long day.
At home, when they've both had a bite to eat,
Her man sits, in his favourite seat,
And drinks his tea from a big china mug.
She sits, for warmth, on the fireside rug.
He reads until it's too dark to see,
She turns her head and leans against his knee.
Bending forward as he touches her head
'Come on you, it's time to go to bed.
You're all tired out, and need your sleep,
After helping, today, with all those sheep.'
Standing, she lovingly sees him go.
Quietly, watches him turn by the door
And smile to see her in the firelight,
Wagging her tail at him, to say - Goodnight!

Haidee Williams

Under The Panama

Under the Panama are sweet thoughts of you
Dressed in a heavenly shade of blue

The time when we met on a warm spring day
In the best month of all - glorious May
Under the Panama are memories of you, looking
so radiant in white

The day when we wed in the month of June,
on the longest day in bright sunlight
Under the Panama I see you in green, looking
modest and mild.

Walking along by the riverside, hand in hand
with out precious child
Moonlight becomes you, your all dressed in
gold under the stars where you sat
Although my hair's silver I want you to
know, I'll never get rid of my
Panama hat.

J M Greves

No Bones About It

An alsation, on his return,
Home one night,
To 'London transport',
A letter did write.

Pointing out,
With great endeavour,
That he had come,
To the end of his tether.

Because, everytime,
He travelled on the underground,
There were no empty seats,
To be found.

As, all the carriages,
If your please,
Were jam-packed,
With the Pekinese.

And he went,
On to say,
In a very nasty,
Sort of way.

If they didn't do something,
At the double,
There was going to be,
A lot of trouble.

Well, just about,
A week went by,
Then they came back,
With this reply.

'We've received your letter,
Of dissatisfaction,
But don't feel inclined,
To take any action.'

'There's really no need,
For your stresses and strains,
Just avoid the 'Peke-hours'
When you use our trains!'

Joe Bayford

Homeland

The only time I feel as one
Is in the warmth of a foreign sun,
To be in this land of native tribes
I feel my mind come alive,
To hear them speak in their native tongue
I feel in my heart a song is sung,
To be in this land I feel whole
In this place I can free my Arabian soul.

Vannesa Fitzgerald

Cathedral Visit

To sing in a cathedral
Is the biggest thrill of all,
Even though the journey there
May be a longish haul!

Blackburn, Lichfield, Worcester,
Cathedrals great and tall,
Have happy memories for me,
As I've sat there in a stall.

Sopranos, altos, tenors, basses,
And often trebles too,
Unite to sing in sacred song,
At the conductor's cue.

Their voices blend in harmony,
The organ joins in too,
To give to God Almighty praise,
Which in His rightful due.

Margaret Patterson

Woodland Walk

There's another world just down the lane and through the woods
where my dog, Ted, takes me to walk each day,
at early hour when I'm still greeting consciousness,
and trying to make the cobwebs go away.
And when Ted's full of energy and hope again
of following the trails which we explore,
while sharing and enjoying quiet companionship,
and finding secrets held in nature's store.

When Ted goes chasing up the slopes and down again,
then splashing through the trickling, twisting brook;
while I am climbing up the path at steadier pace
then standing still to listen and to look
at tree clad hills which seem to reach for passing clouds,
then tumble down to look for hidden roots
or at the majesty of lofty oak and pine
and sprightly silver birch with greening shoots.

Then Ted leads on, and down we go to scramble through
a carpet thick of mouldering fallen leaves;
dodging branches scenting recent squirrel tracks
around a stump, where frosty lichen weaves.
We start to climb again and meet a gentle sun,
which casts its slanting rays between the trees.
Pale yellow fingers splay across the shadows there -
they flicker as though pulsing for release.

Ah! Smell that tantalising waft of burning logs,
nostalgic childhood memories to evoke,
of kneeling by a farmhouse kitchen range to watch
the leaping sparks paint pictures in the smoke.
But now I see a hazy, dancing spiral rise,
and hear the sound of foresters at work.
Ecstatic Ted makes tunnels through the undergrowth,
where many hidden canine fancies lurk.

Beside my feet a bramble clutches grassy tufts
festooned with scintillating, dewy beads;
sheltering protecting beneath its thorny arms,
a lively growing nursery of seeds.
Thus abounds this miracle everywhere I look -
awakening, in every living thing
from winter's restful sleep, which builds the strength to greet
the eager voice of young rejoicing spring.

Ted and I have both braved the bitter winds and snow.
We gladly claimed this transformed world which gives
to root and bud, bird and beast, and to man himself
that magic call when new-born promise lives.
So Ted gambols on with imaginary prey,
or comes running up with treasures to bring
and as I watch I laugh, for still in his first year
this pup himself is heralding the spring.

Catherine Clough

AD, So That's What's The Matter With Me

My doctor has a saying, I've been hearing it for years
He uses it a lot to me and it no longer cheers
No matter what I tell him I just hear this mournful cry
'There's nothing I can do for you, it's Anno Domini'.

I turned up at the surgery, my body racked with pain
He took my notes and read them, then he read them all again
He looked at me and scratched his head, then murmured with a sigh
'You'll have to learn to live with it, it's Anno Domini'.

My wife arrived one morning for the first time in a year
She told him all her symptoms, in her eye a furtive tear
He said, 'There's lots of it about and I'm afraid that I
Can't do a lot to help you dear, it's Anno Domini'.

Asthmatic wheezes, coughs, and sneezes, spots before the eyes
Pimples on your belly, cellulite all round your thighs
Insomnia, neuralgia, even blisters on your bum
'Sorry, I can't help, it's Anno Domini, old chum'.

My little grandchild Annie, one day began to choke
I put her in the car and rushed her to the doctor bloke
He put his finger down her throat, then said, 'I'll have you know
I've found the cause of all that fuss, it's Annie's domino'.

Joe Silver

The Auction

'If you tell the time by Christmas,
You shall have a silver watch,'
Wilfred's freckles merged with dimples
Large blue eyes and golden hair,
They stood him high above his siblings
On Father's carved oak wooden chair
'It's half past daytime, playtime, lifetime'
While the winter wind was howling, snowing,
Time ticked past, slowly going

Polished buttons sewn on khaki
Polished boots in Flanders mud
And all the poppy seeds were blowing,
Growing in the English blood.
Then flew the bullet with his name on
Among the thousands, scything, mowing.
Still loudly ticked the silver watch
And time was going, going.

The little parcel sent to England
With his watch and Mother's letters
Lay fifty years atop the wardrobe
With a medal from his betters
Till his widowed sister Alice
Auctioned off the dusty household
Watched the hammer held on high
'I'm bid ten pounds.' She blocked a memory
Swallowed hard and wiped an eye
Wilfred's watch went for a song
Time ticked, going, going, gone.

E V Fox

Thoughts Of Childhood

As twilight creeps silently into my room
And I sit all alone, the enveloping gloom
Stirs up memories of childhood, and in wakeful dreams
I recall the old cottage with broad oaken beams.

This is the door that led into the hall
Where the gleaming brass warming-pan hung on the wall.
Here in the corner the measured tick-tock
And the dearly loved face of the grandfather clock.

This is the room where we sat down to meals.
I hear parents chatter - I hear our soft squeals
Of delight when dear Bruno had nuzzled our knees
As if to say, 'I'm here, I want my share please.'

The cheery coal fire on a dull winter's day,
Stools drawn up around it for children at play.
Snakes and ladders and dominos, draughts and I spy.
All these things I now see through my mind's inward eye.

In fancy, I see once again my small bed.
Where I'd drawn up the coverlet over my head.
In fear of the dark and not daring to peep.
And oh how I prayed that I'd soon fall asleep.

Here on the wall are the marks which had shown
How much taller each year we young children had grown.
I open a book to find faded and pressed
The tiny wild flowers which small hands once caressed.

And now that I'm old how I wish more and more
That again I could enter that old cottage door.
Leading into the hall where the grandfather clock
Had welcomed us home with its cheerful tick-tock.

C White

Why Darling

Why do I write poetry darling?
It activates my Brain
A line appears in my head
Oh here I go again!

Dusters lay abandoned
When picking up my pen
Promising to clean the house
I really don't know When!

Another thing about it darling
It keeps me rather trim
One refrains from eating junk food
The skirt now fits I'm in

Writing brings about Emotions
Buried deep within my mind
Cleansing heart and soul
A therapy I find

One's inner thoughts darling
Are personal you see
Putting pen to paper
Helps to find the Real me
Hic! Would *you* like a swig darling?

Pamela Brown

Anglian Skies

Anglian skies so high and so wide
Streaked with a finger of grey;
Wild birds a flutter and soaring aloft
To welcome the dawn of the day.

Anglian skies afire with the glow
Of a radiant orange-heart sun:
Miles you can see across the brown land
Where foxes and wild deer do run.

Anglian skies with glorious clouds
Of which they are second to none,
With mountains of cotton wool high in the sky
Silver lined in the rays of the sun.

Anglian skies a panorama of light
Glowing and changing at will
Turning to storm clouds and shafts of dark night
To kaleidoscope rainbows - and 'still'.

With echoes of thunder and rumbles all gone
Away in the distance so far
The skies return to their wondrous sight
With none to equal or par.

Anglian skies, when twilight comes
Turn mystic with orange hue,
Silhouettes dancing across the dark sky
As greens turn to midnight blue.

Anglian skies and polar north light
Myriad stars twinkling above;
North, West or South - none can compare
To these - the skies that I love!

Mollie D Earl

Cushions

Don't you just love cushions
With their squidgy soft insides.
They come in a range of colours,
And some are the same both sides.

You can lean on them, or lie on them,
Or press them into your back.
You can sit on them if you're not very tall,
Few usages they lack.

Some come with fancy tassels,
Some are made with a fringe.
But what I love most, as I'm sure you agree,
Is the way they get rid of a twinge.

Then, when you've lounged around on them
And they've changed their shape to flat,
You can easily fluff them up again
To make them look lusciously fat.

Val Rigby

Memories Past!

Play the music and I am home
Hear its precious sounds so well known
Visualising a way of life so long gone
Days of laughter when sunrays shone
Life's pleasures who's vigour created a dome
Its power engulfing all of my own
Thus I indulge when memories come
And relive my life once lived in the sun.

K Jambor

Eden

Tread not here with human foot
For this is holy ground
This is my Eden, my England,
my home
Where I can walk my fields alone
Where the grass grows tall and the
wind blows free
And the angels stop and talk to me
Where the crows can chat and sit
around
In air unpolluted by human sound,
Where the rabbits play and the
nightingales sing
And the cuckoo comes to visit
in spring
Where the lilacs bloom and the
damsons grow
And the silence speaks when the
sun sets low.

Doris Ginsberg

She Wrote Me A Letter

'You know, the marriage bureau thought us
suitable material,
but you approach life like a tortoise.
Our engagement's one long serial!

You said I was your 'clinging petal'
but with all your dithering
I feel like a stinging nettle
and my flowers are withering!

I guess you could say we're together,
but why am I still dating, for
I've asked myself each moment whether
life with you's worth waiting for!

I know you mean well, for you're trying
very hard to get employment,
but when you're sitting all day sighing
where on earth is my enjoyment?

I've only had one moment's laughter,
when you broke your leg out skating.
Could we be 'Happy ever after?'
Maybe, if you are emigrating!

One day perhaps if you're deciding
that marriage is your proposition,
I'd be quite happy just providing
unquestioned total opposition!

Don't ring me, write or try to find me
or ask for further explanations.
I'm leaving life with you behind me,
forever severing relations!'

John Christopher

A Romany Man

Along the road I travelled on
With horse and cart and in song;
O what a lovely life I lead,
A man of the road and a Romany.

Long weary miles I have roamed
With my horse and vardo for a home;
Many friends I've met here and there
Who for one another always care.

Highways, byways, come and go
As we find a place to set up home;
By the campfire we eat our scran.
It feels great to be a Romany man.

As soon as we have settled down
Along comes the law from the town.
We are then told we must move on;
What on this earth have we done?

Oh Lord we have done no-one harm;
We are a people who live calm,
Who want to live and roam this land
Conducting our lives the best we can.

After hitching up on the move again,
Along the road we make our way.
Where can we go in this dear land
To find a place for the travelling man.

I wish we could go back in time
When life for travellers was no crime,
No hate or malice would you find
From Romany folk or their kind.

If only we could travel in peace
From North to South, West to East,
And we could live in this dear land
The peaceful life of a Romany man.

Francis Allen

I Am Fine Thank You

There's nothing the matter with me
I'm as healthy as can be
I have arthritis in both knees
When I talk, it's with a wheeze!
My pulse is weak, my blood is thin
But I'm awfully well for the shape I'm in
Arch supports I have for my feet,
Or I wouldn't be out in the street,
Sleep is denied me night after night,
But every morning I'm usually all right.
My memory's failing, my head's in a spin
But I'm awfully well for the shape I'm in.
The moral is this, as my tale I unfold
That for those of us who are growing old.
It's better to say 'I'm fine!' With a grin
Than to let folks know the shape we are in
How do I know my youth is all spent?
Well my 'get up and go' has got up and went
Old age is golden, I've heard it said
But, sometimes I wonder as I get into bed
My ears in the drawer, my teeth in a cup.
My eyes on the table, until I wake up.
'Ere sleep overtakes me, I say to myself,
'Is there anything left to put on the shelf?'
Now when I was young, my slippers were red
I could kick my heels over my head!
When I got older my slippers were blue,
But still I could dance the whole night through,
Now I am old my slippers are black
I walk to the store, and puff my way back.

B Clark

Fred The Butcher's Mighty Roar

The birds of prey all took to flight,
Flamingos filled the sky,
Chameleons then hid from sight
While fear filled the eye.

Some crocodiles sort safety deep
One hippo raised its head,
A leopard stopped its silent creep,
What could it be they dread?

Elephants raged with loss of face
While monkeys shook the trees,
Then cheetahs fled with quicker pace
As rhinos shook their knees.

The zebras cast up clouds of dust
Gazelles were fleeing too!
A place of safety seemed a must
As thunder shook their view.

A pride of lions proud no more
In silence left the scene,
For Fred the butcher's mighty roar
Had turned their pride to green.

Fred's famous voice had travelled far,
Had travelled far I say!
Through jungle deep to Zanzibar
From Manchester that day!

Peter James O'Rourke

Food For Thought

Can we not stop and think
What it is we eat and drink,
Wine beer chicken chips
Mmm, just lick your lips,
Crisps scones lemonade
Looks like you need first aid,
Caviar and pork pies
Eat until your stomach cries,
Ah what's the fuss anyway
We'll all be going home someday,
So eat what you can
Drink what you will
For all we have is time to kill.

William Brand

Lauren

Walking 'round in those high heels
My mother, she tries to be.
Puts lipstick on those cupid lips
And chatters constantly!
In her mind, she's adult now
But we all see for real.
Puppy-dog eyes, so innocent,
Life's emotions yet to feel.
Makes me feel like I'm the child
Reprimanding me each day.
To see the learning through those eyes,
She takes my breath away,
Those tiny steps of wisdom
Makes this gift my life.
Undying love cannot say enough,
It hurts to hear her cry.
'Your time, right now, is yours to keep,
I gaze in wonder as you sleep.
Will this love we have still be the same
When the time arrives to make your way?
Lauren, time is precious,
Sweet life tastes so delicious.
Your race is on, before you've begun,
You're way ahead of everyone!'

Caroline Sammout

The Dress

It was a beautiful floating dress of pink
Lined, and patterned with roses; I think?
I loved the flimsy skirt with the delicate swirl
It was a fairy-tale dress, to a little girl
On a hanger, in the wardrobe, hung on the rack
Brought out to be looked at, then put safely back
I knew it was special, 'cos Mam loved it as well
She gazed at it fondly; that's how I could tell
Sadly, I only saw it every now and then
The Very last time Ever, was when I was ten
It was laid on the floor, on a sheet, safe from dirt
With a Great Big Piece cut out of the skirt!
'What have you done, what's happened?' I cried
'I need muslin, to sieve flour, to make bread' Mam sighed!
It was wartime you see, the flour wasn't pure
So she wanted to sieve it, just to make sure
That no harm would come to my brothers and me
When we sat down to eat the bread for our tea
People couldn't just go to a shopping parade
The bread in those days, was always home made
My Mother must truly have loved us; I guess
For she gave up her cherished, 'Pink Voile Wedding Dress'.

E Warlow

Farewell To A Memory

The garden gate hangs broken, its hinges red with rust,
The step, once white, is grey now with all the gathering dust;
The crazy-paving once so neat, is overgrown with grass,
The straggling rose around the door is difficult to pass.
The windows once so sparkling clean, are black with dirt and grime,
Showing how they've suffered from the ravages of time.
The cherry tree no longer stands, its boughs a heap of wood,
What happy times upon its swing I spent in my childhood.
The garden's like a jungle, its plants choked by the weeds,
No fragrant flowers bloom in the sun - a sorry sight indeed;
Folk say it is an eyesore, and view it with a frown,
I felt I must have one last look before they pull it down.
Soon the workmen will arrive, demolish with no trouble,
They'll cart away my memories along with all the rubble.
I begin to wish I had not come, for nothing stays the same,
Trying to put back the clock is just a foolish game;
I haven't heard what will replace this house so dear to me,
I hope it's something useful, something nice to see.
I won't be coming back again, the pain would be too strong,
But my house will still be in my dreams where memories belong.

Kathleen Poulton

If Only

If only there were more trees
Birds, deer and bees,
The land would be so pretty
But it would be such a pity,
If there were none of these.

If only there were less roads
That do hurt badgers and toads,
There would be less pollution
So if we found a good solution,
And all made a 'no' ode.

If only the sky was brighter
My life would be much mightier,
You could sing and dance and jump around,
Whilst listening to birds beautiful sound,
The rain would come down lighter.

If only plants were 'more of'
And grass and bushes 'heard of',
The land would be so pretty
But it would such a pity,
If there were none of these.

Amii Nettleingham

The Amateur Photographer

I love to see the seagulls
Catching stale and soggy bread.
Wheeling, diving, screeching,
As they fly over my head.
My arms resting on the railings
Of the river promenade.
My camera at the ready
For me to press the shutter hard,
As they come in to take the bait
I click!
As always - just too late!

Perhaps I should have another try
And wind the film along,
The gulls are hungry, they will wait,
I can't possibly go wrong.
A second try - then on and on -
Until the film is finished, done.
No final try. No other shot.
The wretched birds cannot be got.
How can I win the club trophy?
It seems my fate is not to be
The winner of the comp.

Nancy K Kiberd

Sectarian Prayers

I saw the hard men drilling men
Teaching them how to kill.
I saw the trained men killing men
Using their fresh learnt skill.

I saw the sad girls kissing men,
Tearfully goodbye-ing,
I saw them grieve for missing men;
Dead men and men dying.

I watched the 'fire bomb' making men
Throwing their deadly flame,
All sanity forsaking men,
All decency and shame.

I saw and heard the preaching men
Lamenting the young dead,
And mothers all beseeching men
To pray for peace instead.

When all sides paused from slaying then
Their hands washed clean of blood
They knelt in church with praying men
As all good Christians should.

Jack Macfarlane

Autumn Whispers

Nature bares, her wholesome fruit
fields of gold, fields of wheat,
farmers happy with their yield
sing and whistle, sing and wield.

Birds in treetops with chorus strong
sing with praises, humble song,
leaves change colour flutter down
russet red, golden brown.

Squirrels hoard their winter store
busy hoarding, searching more,
breezes whistle through the trees
winter's coming, hurry please.

Underfoot the dry leaves crunch
beetles scurry, hedgehogs lunch,
autumn golds the colours bright
leaves are falling, swallows flight.

Clouds are rolling in the sky
smoky, misty, sweeping by.
A transformation's taking place
autumn whispers, hurry make haste.

J Williams

Fishtales!

Fishermen with weathered hands,
Mending nets on golden sands.
Telling stories of the sea,
Conjuring images for me.

They tell me of the porpoises,
That leap, and laugh, and prance.
Of seals that pop their heads up,
Like old men at a dance.

The crabs that all walk sideways,
Of hermit ones that hide.
The brown and crinkly seaweed,
That comes in on the tide.

A lobster with its pincers,
The hammerhead shark.
Catfish with its whiskers.
The dogfish with no bark.

Jaunty bobbing fishing boats,
Each bears a special name.
So different in their dressing,
Though at first they look the same.

Those proud and valiant fishermen,
A rare exclusive band.
So at home upon the sea.
Fish out of water on the land.

Joan Enefer

Love

Love is wiping away the tears,
Love is being there all the years.
Love is sharing the joy,
Love is there to give to girl or boy.
Love is there when we fall,
Love helps us once again stand tall.
Love brings us gifts to share,
Love takes time to choose them with such flair,
Love stays around when we are old,
Love cares for us when in sickness we are told.
Love is there until we die,
Love we can count on until we say our last goodbye.

Jean Rendell

The Daffodil

'Don't hurt my dress,' The daffodil made sounds,
As weedkiller was scattered all around,
Which fell upon her yellow trumpet folds,
Devouring slowly working through the rolled,
And fluted skirt, whilst fearfully she frowned.

She quivered as the afternoon sun crowned,
About her face upraised which felt the pound,
Of another acrid drop amidst her scold,
'Don't hurt my dress,'

Her withered gown clung limply to the ground,
Where listlessly she slumped upon her mound,
Of long-grass as iife drained whilst she grew cold,
And at the last dying anguish tolled,
In breathy whispers, faint and barely found,
'Don't hurt my dress!'

Aileen Hopkins

The Snowdrops

Snowdrops while the days are warm,
rest in peace in earth below.
Sheltered from the waving blades,
of tender grass that ebb and flow.

Throughout the pleasant summer months,
bulbs so small and weak,
gather strength from fertile soil,
primed for winter cold and bleak.

Rain is lashing, wind is rising,
vegetation dead and dying.
Ground is icy, bulbs are stirring,
flowers for the light are yearning.

Snowdrops while the days are dark,
display their shapely heads.
Nodding proudly in the breeze,
in frost bound winter beds.

Throughout those lengthy winter months,
they brighten up the stage,
jewels twinkling like the stars,
cultured from a bygone age.

Alwyn James

Nature Is Such A Wonderful Thing

The way that nature is such a wonderful thing,
the way that the flowers bloom, and the birds sing,
the way the warm sun, and the cool winds caress,
the way the creatures of the world draw breath,
the way the plants and trees just grow and grow,
the way that the rivers and lakes ebb and flow,
the way that snow and rain will fall with grace,
the way that planet Earth turns endlessly in space,
the way that mountains and hills stand proud, so high,
the way they compliment the clouds within the sky,
the way that the sea and oceans are so very deep,
the way the starry sky passes you by, as your sleep,
the way each fresh morning, a brand new day is born,
the way the bright sunlight welcomes another dawn.

Christopher Higgins

This Wondrous World

The roosters all crowing at the outbreak of dawn
The world all awakening as a new day is born
Now born babies arriving as old people go
The wheels of evolution are seen in full flow

The world is so wonderful and strange in its ways
With all of its miracles that are seen every day
The sun in the morning providing the light
And the moon and the stars taking over at night

But God has created those things that we treasure
With the snow and the rain and warm days of pleasure
The rivers all flowing to the wide open seas
Whilst the trees and the flowers all bend in the breeze

The mountains all reaching far into the sky
Towering like sentinels way up there on high
We should treat all those things with the best of respect
Don't let them be ignored or fall into neglect.

Lachlan Taylor

Somewhere A Rose Is Blooming

(For Jan)

The meaning in Brahms' little tune
Recalls from Sussex long ago
A village shimmering in the noon-
Day summer warmth and love's first glow;

Recalls from Sussex long ago
An age-old pub and wandering street,
Day-summer warmth and love's first glow
And hand-hold in a kindling heat,

An age-old pub and wandering street,
A Saxon church in honeyed stone
And hand-hold in a kindling heat,
Then kisses snatched while we're alone.

A Saxon church in honeyed stone,
Grave monuments of lugubrious words
Then kisses snatched while we're alone
Between the church path's stone-edged curbs.

Grave monuments of lugubrious words
Meant nothing to us in those days
Between the church path's stone-edged curbs.
That time that grants always repays

Meant nothing to us. In those days
We loved and let our passions burn.
That time that grants always repays
Was lessons we had yet to learn.

We loved and let our passions burn
The years gone by. How ageing shames
Was lessons we had yet to learn;
While passion dies, real love reclaims

The years gone by. How ageing shames
A village shimmering in the noon!
While passion dies, real love reclaims
The meaning in Brahms' little tune.

John H Hope

A Famous Three

A famous three now comes to mind -
For this is a task that has been assigned.
Kipling, Tennyson and Long-fellow
Wrote their poetry deep and mel-low.

To have any image in words poured out
Needs concentration and thinking about.
The image exceeds all expectation -
Magnifying one's imagination.

Deceptive words of darkness and light
Bringing the content into our 'sight'
And forming the picture in the Poet's mind
As he pens his words to awaken the 'blind'.

These thoughtful folk now come to mind -
I wish I could write them a letter -
But I will read these famous three
For I'd like to know them better.

Pat Melbourn

Living On The Fringes

The loners come to crowded places
so they can see other faces.
Lost in the crowd they secretly wish,
for love, bliss, lost family connections,
romance, caring, warm embraces and sharing.
A sense of belonging, their deepest longing.

Tossed into a world of throwaway toys,
disposables, recyclables, computerised noise.
Interchangeable, rearrangable, human parts
It's no wonder they feel dehumanised in their hearts.

The question remains for one and the same,
those who are players against their will at life's game.
Are they the losers at life, or did fate step in,
to change their direction so they would look within?

Through each window they peek, outsiders still,
in hopes for redemption, disconnected to be resurrected.
Their punishment harsh and truly unjust,
they didn't really ask for too much.
No, they didn't ask to be a loner in a crowd,
just another loner in a crowd.

Myra Rigor Selvadurai

A Midsummer Night's Dream

Once upon a time My Darling
On a bright clear sunny morn
When the dew was on the meadow
There were toadstools on the lawn.

They were growing in a circle
Some were yellow some were red
This is where the fairies gathered
Dancing while I lay in bed.

When the moon was shining brightly
Shining with her silver light
I crept down the winding staircase
In the middle of the night.

Down I crept my bare feet treading
So I did not make a sound
Out onto the lawn I hastened
There was dew upon the ground.

Then I saw them oh my darling
Such a sight I've never seen
Fairies dancing in the moonlight
Surely this must be a dream

Still they danced and still I watched them
But the moon was on her way
Then a cock crowed shrilling loudly
Heralding the break of day.

So the dancing now was ended
Fairies gathering up the dew
Treading lightly on the toadstools
Standing poised then off they flew.

Sylvia Bryan

London

England's green and pleasant land
Has a story, proud and grand!
London too has quite a story,
Centre once of Empire's glory!

Through the gates of this great port
Came the migrants, every sort,
Who helped to make this city great,
A Centre for trade, a route for freight.

London flourished through the ages,
Centre of wealth and home for sages.
Every sort of refugee
Found a welcome here you see!

They brought their skill; they brought their drive;
They brought their joy to be alive
And though it was a crowded place,
Everyone was found a space!

Huguenots, but Catholics too,
The Moslem, welcome as the Jew!
Black and brown, as well as white,
Given hope whate'er their plight.

Here in harmony they live;
So much that's past, so much to give,
Yet, whatever point of view,
Now they all are British too!

And all the languages they speak,
Too much to learn, too far to seek,
English now's their common tongue
For everything that's said or sung!

Patrick Davies

Plastic Freedom

A number or a type
To accompany your life
Visa, Mastercard, Amex, Switch or Delta,
The cards of today, and of the future.

Use them to purchase anything
Even 'Junk' - of course, providing -
You have the necessary in the 'bank'
To meet your repayments with thanks.

It's the way of life
For man and wife
Be pleased to say
We can pay this way.

Our funeral expenses
We are considering now
Before we take
Our final bow.

All paid up,
This 'Plastic Freedom'
We are sure will continue
Beyond the 'Millennium'.

M Jenks

Compensations

Lorries, who speed, then hold you up and make you fume,
The sweetest memory resurrected by a half forgotten tune:
Drivers, who cut you up and grin and think they're smart,
Long legged schoolgirls, on their way to class:
Terrorists, of every flavour, hue or creed,
Princess Leia, Katy Manning, Purdy and Steed.

Smug female clerics, with gleeful faces,
Eyes of forget-me-not blue so deep:
People, who spit in public places,
Classical music to make you weep:
Fat foul-mouthed feminists, full of bile and spleen,
Memories of Elvis and Norma Jean.

Disease and illness, mortality, ugliness and death,
The tranquillity and peace of a redeeming Angels' breath:
Plumbers and builders, who let you down and cheat,
The innocence and joy of the daily 'Page Three' treat:
The rich emotional intensity of a Bruch or Brahms,
The soft safe sweetness of a lover's arms.

Dealers of every kind, who sell you high and buy too low,
The Last Night of the Proms (again!); the first bluebell:
Bullying, violence, militancy, 'PC' and woe,
The generous heart and smile of a kind young girl:
The unwelcome stridency of 'gays', who think us queer,
Art, literature, music, 'magic moments', ginger beer!

Conflict, aggravation, stress and strife,
Superman, Star Trek, Mindy and Mork:
The perturbations in our daily life,
'Made glorious summer by this Son of York'!
The compensations of even just an average day,
Are consolations they by far outweigh.

Anthony G Webster

The Squirrel

I cannot help but love you for grace and charm and wit,
your cautious, jerky movements, arms folded when you sit.

You keep watch on the garden while resting on the post,
and flick your tail in warning; 'That is *my* piece of toast.'

Running towards your target with undulating gait,
your tail flows out behind you, like thistledown in weight.

Burnt toast is clasped in forepaws just like a hazel nut,
so quickly gnawed and swallowed; passed down into your gut.

Now for the peanut feeder which hangs down from a tree,
you gaze up to assess the case. The problem you can see.

But can you solve it squirrel? Can you outwit my scheme
to keep the nuts for bluetits, you acrobatic dream?

Persistence is your middle name, sharp teeth tools of your trade,
you're happy hanging upside down; your courage does not fade.

You leave it for the moment; I've won first round I know.
But you'll be back to try again and all my nuts will go.

Fruit trees are now your playground; leaping from branch to branch,
testing our pears for ripeness, choosing the best for lunch.

I love you and I hate you! I don't know what to feel.
Destroyer, killer, acrobat; you entertain but steal.

Wendy S Allen

The Final Solution

Why is it dear do you suppose
I cannot sleep at night.
Those dreams I have of sweet repose
Are swiftly put to flight.

As soon as I put out the light
Or so it seems to me,
The snoring starts and once again
To the spare room I flee.

Oh heart of mine you are divine
But sweet talk's wearing thin
'cause even with the ear plugs, dear
I still can hear the din.

So I'm afraid the end is nigh,
I'm going to visit Mum.
When I come home if you still snore
The last resort's a gun!

Paddy Jupp

Golden Sun

The golden sun is beating down
Upon the brown and arid ground
The heat is rising from the dale
'Tis summer on the greatest scale

The steamy heat upon my brow
Cheer up my love - 'tis summer now
And everybody fills with cheer
The sky is blue, the day is clear

For when the clouds shall form again
And the rivers fill with rain
And lilies float upon the pond
And hail the beauty of the swan

Triumphant is the golden sun
Another summer's day is done
No finer sight could one achieve
Than that of wondrous summer's eve.

David John Dunbar

Neucosis

Is no need for neurosis
Cause I have a deep psychosis
Not afraid of any trees
But hate stinging by the bees

Never puts me up in bed
But there's trouble in the head
Went to the shrink a little late
Hope to get my head on straight

Set and talk quite a while
He will frown when I smile
Guess he has an awesome power
Gettin' hundred bucks an hour

That good doctor really tried
Told a tale, then he lied
Is no way I benefited
Cause that shrink is now committed

George E Statham

Daddy Christmas

I like Christmas, it gives me joy,
Too be a girl, and not a boy,
To hang my stocking by the bed,
And hope the note I sent's been read.

To go to bed, when mamma tells
And hope to hear the sound of bells,
His special trip from the North Pole,
Just to bring my talking doll.

The chimney waits, the fires out,
In case Santa is about,
Cause he comes down it as a rule,
And so he likes it kept quite cool,

I move the covers take a peek,
In time to see old Santa creep,
I now know, and I am glad,
Cause I know really, it's good old dad.

J Bright

The Wind

The wind it said to me one day
Would you like to come and play

You can bring your kite and let it go
I'll make it dance put on a show

For all the kids below to watch
I'll make it jump and do hop-scotch

Up among the clouds so high
Watching all the world go by

Up and up, and up it soared
All the children, they laughed and roared

It's bedtime now the wind did say
I hope you'll come again and play

A Fidler

The Club

Hail, rain, wind and snow
To Eston Labour Club, we will go
John, George and Margaret, sell the flyers and books
Gill has no duty, you should see the looks
Jimmy's the treasurer, I know where he's been
To water the plants, for the secretary, Jean
Mick's on the raffle, the raffle, again
Whenever you see him, he's on two 'till ten
Who's calling bingo, it must be Jeanette
Change her, for Tommy. She's unlucky pet
Brenda, asked Ann, if she'd do the tote
I will, in a minute, when I take off my coat
Here comes Lyndsey, across the dance floor
He's taking the cover charge, on the door
Ernie, the chairman, in the office, he's been
Counting, takings, with the secretary, Jean
Tony's, the games secretary
There's games in the bar
That, reminds me, he owes me a jar
Gordon, and Leslie, the steward and stewardess
Fred and Alma's relieved them
They have gone, to Loch Ness
My poem is written, I may, write again
But not, at the moment
There's no ink, in my pen.

Peter Edward Waines Briggs

Seasons Of The Year

Curtains of alabaster snow drifting from a grey, ambient sky
Icicles glistening on sheltered houses, nearby
Silhouettes of trees playing a concerto with the imagination
Animals running over cold fields, looking for a safe destination
Happy, enchanted children, in layers and layers of clothes
In a red little face, shines a red little nose
In anticipation, their mouth open wide
Excited voices ever so bright - it's winter, it's winter

Awakening of feelings, of aroused emotions
Weeping willows shake of coats of white, with a knowing notion
Tiny green heads popping through rugged grass, awaited by a soft lawn
Proud animal-mothers show their offspring, to a misty dawn
Fauna and flora awake, the birds are singing
First glances of love, don't know what the season will be bringing
Rosy babies on their mother's arms,
Raise their tiny voices in a unison of charm - it's spring, it's spring.

Hot, humid, air, rays glowing from a clear, blue sky
People worshipping the sun, life is on a high
Rippling sea of yellow fields, waiting for cool morning rains
Children, away from sweltering heat, laughing, making daisy-chains
Dogs trotting along, with hanging tongues, to tired to retrieve
Delusions of immortality, ever just so brief
Passions collide, like a film in slow motion
Everything is done, without any devotion
Nature looks bright and shiny and well
In the distance you can hear noises swell - it's summer, it's summer.

Brown leaves are falling from a tired, bended tree
Majestic swans, flying off, across the sea
Little squirrels collect the last nuts, with haste
Everything has a sweet bitter taste
Hazy, golden sunshine brings forgotten feelings of things to
come
Light warm breezes rush through barns of hay, with a
whispering hum
Everyone gets ready for something unknown
The circle of nature is fulfilled, it's closing down
But everything in life is done for a purpose, for a reason
Nothing ever will change, it's just the end of the season - it's
autumn, it's autumn.

Ingrid Bockmann

A Poet's Poem

Many a day I have lost my vision
and walked in vain down insperation street
With nothing but a worn out smile
and some brand new shoes upon my feet

Many a day I have gone to the church
where the preacher is a poet the same as me
we sit in prayer and wait for the words
but the words have no meaning as far as I can see

Once or twice I have gone to the station
and talked with the man who lives in the booth
once I asked him where to find inspiration
and he said; my inspiration lives up on the roof

So up on the roof I stole his passion
but found that the words had less mind than my own
when I left that place I was not disheartened
because I found that my vision and feeling had grown

Many a time my pen has found bounty
in words on the surface about hearing and sight
but these words have no meaning if they do not go deeper
and with this in my mind my pen does take flight

Teri Perkins

Butterflies

Flutter, flutter, flutter by
Pretty little butterfly
Sometimes one and sometimes two
Sometimes periwinkle blue
Red Admirals becoming rare
But yesterday I spied a pair
Then suddenly as if to please
One came and landed on my sleeve
Showing off its colours gay
Then soon it fluttered on its way
I'm coming to the firm conclusion
That Cabbage Whites breed in profusion
On my lavender are swarming
All arrive without much warning
Spending hours and hours at play
On this sunny August day
To choose the patio some find fun
With wings outstretched bask in the sun
But when dark clouds a visit pay
Those butterflies just slip away
Though the flowerbeds live with colour
But how much we miss the other
Coloured wings so full of movement
Nature couldn't make improvement
In that delicate design
Coloured patterns O so fine
Tortoiseshell and Peacock too
And many of a different hue
You see them all between the showers
Visiting a million flowers.

Peter Hugh Bennett

Rain

Trickling, gliding
Slipping, sliding
Rounded pearls
Making swirls
Rushing down
Ceaseless rain
Delicately caressing
My windowpane

D Meek

My Secret Garden

In my secret garden
love is my warden
surrounded by peace,
all wars forever to cease

A newly painted front gate
forbids the entrance of hate
death and disease would fall,
if they tried to climb my wall

I could convert thieves,
into trees, with an abundance of leaves,
enhanced by decorative pillars,
transformed from potential killers

In total elimination
of racial discrimination,
colourful flowers
replace maniacal powers

My secret garden
would serve to pardon
frailties of the human population,
to create a world bubbling with elation

And I would throw in a stream
by which one could dream

Christine Clayton-Owen

Night Sky

Blackest velvet, jewelled with spangled stars,
    rosy Venus, Jupiter, and Mars.
Virgin worlds, in timeless cobalt space,
    endless challenge to the human race.

Fiery comet streaks across the sky,
    someone is born, another is to die.
Silver paths of the milky way,
    like handfuls of stardust tossed away.

Soon dawn's pageant will unfold,
    rose and silver, blue and gold,
but till then night's silver glow,
    caresses sleeping worlds below.

Sheila Giles

For Sophie - Aged Six

It would be good, my dearest child
If I could talk of country wild;
Of gentle fields and woolly sheep
And daisies closing when they sleep

Of silence in a dark green wood
And country people true and good
Lakes, rivers and rippling streams
And on I'd talk in reams and reams.

It would be good but can't be so.
There are other things that you should know.
Worried people out of work,
Stealing in the city murk.

Greyness, concrete, where people live
No loving left for them to give.
Countries fighting, fierce in war,
Yes, my child, there's more and more.

It would be good, my dearest child,
If you could keep your manners mild
Your innocence and gentle ways
Be happy in your early days.

But later, could you be aware
Of others and the pain they bear?
Ugliness and beauty too
Are there to hurt, and soothe you through.

Marge Halling

On Writing In Rhyme

You have asked me to write
A poem in rhyme
But my mind is a blank -
It is most of the time!

Of what shall I write?
I haven't a clue.
Mr Kipling I'm not -
But neither are you!

The world is so full
Of a great many things
So what shall I choose -
Cabbages or kings?

Cabbages are green,
Kings are so rare -
I've never met one
But what do I care?

I'm sure what you seek
Is not such a jingle,
But I'll send it in hope
With laughter you'll tingle!

I shall watch in the post
For rejection slip white -
Great poem this ain't,
But it's been fun to write!

Maria-Christina

Summer

Summer is here - she came today!
Everyone thought she'd lost her way
Amongst the gales and cloudy skies
And heavy rains blinding her eyes.

She trudged doggedly, shrouded in mist,
Anxiously peering at the seasonal list,
Shivering with cold and talking aloud
About the global warming and what clout

It has over today's generation.
And as for ozone layer degradation,
It would be better not to know
What Summer thought on her long crawl.

And so today she arrived at last;
Surveying grey, sad people aghast
And realising how much she was missed,
How loved she was by man and beast.

Wet flowers lifted their heads and smiled
At her as she walked by, warm and kind.
People have found good words for each other
And smiled as well - as if she were Mother.

Glory be to Summer - and thank you for coming.
Spread your favours equally among pleb and king.
And please try to stay for as long as you can.
And next year come sooner, promise? - Done!

Anna Nicol

Hidden Feelings

What is it that I see each day
My life slowly slipping away
Walking along the pathways of life so alone
A lost soul without a home

Feeling pain that is like a knife
Through my heart it goes, taking my life
Draining me by drawing blood
As if to prove that I am not made of wood

What am I going to do?
To stop me feeling so sad and blue
Should I become selfish, unfeeling and cold
Or should I keep my feelings like a secret, never to be told.

Take all the pain that life throws at me
Never ever letting anybody see
Just how much I hate feeling this way
Pretending just to live for today.

Worrying in secret about tomorrow
Feeling all this pain and sorrow
Wanting desperately to break free
Of the burdens that seem to be surrounding me.

Lynn Kilpatrick

January

Shafts of winter sun yellow the trees,
as the ice wind whistles sharp in the breeze.
Water-logged muck where once there was soil,
leafless briers hug a slippery stile.

The dark swollen river races noisily on,
carrying clay, twigs and rubbish along
'till it reaches the tree strangling the way.
In the watery deep, all will slowly decay.

The storm over, damage is done.
Clearing up has just begun.
With arms full of kippeens, I absorb the calm.
Then I heard it . . . the cry of a newborn lamb.

Joan Blake

Sunset

As evenings lull arrives to cushion,
The falling of day into night.
Weary in mind and in body,
I pause to witness this mellow sight.

Hushed beauty, as the sun is setting across the field,
Resplendent in fine amber glow.
Refreshing and healing as gentle spring rain,
As sweet as the roses when soft breezes blow.

So unobstructive, yet so striking,
This brilliant ball of gold.
Yet so quiet, so soothing,
A silent benediction, for all to behold.

Breathing deeply, as if to inhale this warmth and peace,
I find a touch of irony in this I have laid eyes on.
That in a less than ideal world,
There rests perfection on the horizon.

I pray the tender memory of such blessed serenity,
Will stay a while, as in calm certainty I take respite.
Knowing that, there is no better way to close each day,
Then when the earth is kissed such a glorious kiss, goodnight.

Karen Link

Forgotten

Autumn evenings waning fast
And longer were the shadows cast
As she remained alone -
With memories, though faded grown.

The inside window frosted white,
Yet she knew little of that night
Huddled up beneath her shawl.
No one on her did ever call.

Her eyelids closed in deepest slumber.
What else on her could life encumber?
Yet on her face a pleasant smile
As she was with him for awhile.

Upon the table almost bare
A dried up crust. A stray white hair.
A bottle half of curdled milk.
A coat now faded thin as silk.

The ashes in the grate long cold
But of her plight no one was told.
The parlour door no longer shut
A curtain pulled across it, but -
A draught that pierced her to the core.
She knew she couldn't take much more.

As dawn arose she passed away
But none to grieve her on that day.
Yet on her face was shewn no pain
At last she was with him again.

D R Thomas

Dreams

The long dark night, ends with the dawn
The dreams we dreamed, fade with the morn
Now we face another day
Will we falter and lose our way
Bright hopes stir in the human breast
Are we riding on a crest
Oft we rise to fall again
Seems as though we try in vain
Each day has its highs and lows
When all is well, our spirit glows
Man keeps trying to right all wrongs
Nations in their native tongues
Appeal for help, while children starve
Could we but their troubles halve
Will that day come, when dreams come true
The black night past, we see the blue
Of skies without a cloud in sight
The world is now wondrous bright

Kathleen Glover

Birds Of A Feather

On Christmas cards 'mid a winter scene,
This little robin can be seen,
Perched on a branch, or in the snow,
Always knows where he wants to go.

Often seen in a flying stance,
This is the gentle dove,
White in colour, with an olive branch,
It speaks of peace and love.

Watching the soil being turned,
Perched on the garden barrow,
Waiting to catch a lively worm,
This is the cheeky sparrow.

Out in the open countryside,
With a lovely trilling sound,
Wide awake, and bright of eye,
The lark is soaring heaven bound.

Fish for breakfast, this is the start,
From low-hanging branch see him dart,
For lively colours on the riverbank,
Kingfisher is the one to thank.

Often accused of stealing rings,
Coloured beads and other things,
You can put this rumour to rest,
If you look in the jackdaw's nest.

Passing away a winter's hour,
Writing has been fun,
Bringing to you pictures in words,
Now my work is done.

W C Niel

The World

This world to me is a wonderful place
No matter what colour or creed or race
The sky above can be blue or grey
Some places it's night and some places it's day
The valleys and mountains and rivers and seas
The animals and insects the birds and the trees
The city packed tight and the wide open spaces
The millions of people with all different faces
This world is a jewel a gift to treasure
We must make sure we keep it for everyone's pleasure.

Janet Brown

Change

It was a very peaceful village,
Living in that lovely little cottage;
Calmness reigned within no doubt,
Noise and commotion's, no where about.

Moving around quite silently,
Leaving the house discreetly,
In her usual gentle way.
Even her neighbours had nothing to say.

Dreaming all about Jupiter and Mars,
At night-time she gazed at the stars.
Through her window was the Milky Way,
Yes she was content both night and day.

Then one morning her dreams were shattered,
Sightseers and 'Press' at her door battered.
Alas they'd found out her secret address,
Causing confusion and maybe some stress.

Her life now had to change direction,
Silence being a very small section.
Back to the life of bustle and flurry,
Why not, it's a change-always being in a hurry.

Dorothy Whitehall

2000 AD - Embracing The New Millennium

Two thousand years of history -
Continue to create,
Milestones of achievement -
New memories to awake!

Two thousand years of growing -
Those stepping-stones that place,
The spring boards of society -
That have a natural grace!

Two thousand years of learning -
That knowledge makes man free!
Progression and mobility -
From which we cannot flee!

Two thousand years of progress -
Of mankind's drive and toil!
From flintstone to the space age -
Powered by drilling oil!

Two thousand years when nations -
Have fought and spread their wings!
The desire for peace to prosper -
The hope millennium brings!

Two thousand years we celebrate -
When mostly men are free,
To embrace the new millennium -
In two thousand years AD!

Doreen Wheeldon

Hanky Panky In Our Garden

This morning bright and early
Our neighbour called to say
That when he passed our gate last night
He saw the strangest thing
Two lovely coloured foxes
Were playing in our drive
But never even noticed
Our neighbour stood outside
My husband's never seen a fox
So later on that night
He crept out in our garden
And saw this lovely sight.
A fox had found our dustbin
And turned it upside down.
So he could eat some scrapes of food
Upon a grassy mound.
My husband moved in closer then
To get a better view
But triggered off the light we have
Which scared the fox off too.
We also have some badgers
Some squirrels, and rabbits too
That's why we really love it here
I bet that you would too.

Merilyn Gulley

The Death Of A Princess

Oh, dearest Diana, your beauty and your grace
Has captured a world that sometimes seems grey
In the chamber of our hearts we will keep you whole
As a precious gem set in pure gold
You forever young and beautiful will stay
We will always cherish the kindness you displayed
Free from the hounding chase of your every day
In the peace and quiet, forever you will lay.

Birthe McCabe

My Boyfriend Talks In Rhyme

My boyfriend talks in rhyme,
All of the time,
He offered to stop,
For it seemed a little over the top,
But then life seemed strange,
And proved difficult to arrange,
He got in such a tiz,
It nearly ruined his biz
And totally confused the music press,
Life was such a mess,
So now my boyfriend once again,
Even though it is a pain,
Talks (as he did before) in rhyme,
All of the time,
And I am glad,
For it made me sad,
To see him stress,
And be in such a mess,
Over not talking in rhyme,
All of the time.

Tamarisk Kay

Where There's Muck . . .

I'd done me days work digging coal down the pit,
And I sez to meself, sez I,
Before I go home I'll away to the pub,
For me throat is hoarse and dry.

So I took meself off to the inn for a jar,
And such a surprise got I.
For the pub had been refurbished -
Not a minute too soon, sez I.

'Stead of sawdust, a carpet was now on the floor,
And curtains to prettify.
Polished tables and flowery cushions on seats,
Which look very nice, sez I.

So I leaned on the bar and called to mine host,
I sez to the landlord, sez I,
I'll partake of a pint of your best, if you please,
With a slice of your wife's rabbit pie!

Well he looked very sheepish as he approached me;
Couldn't look me straight in the eye.
'I'm afraid I can't serve you in your working clothes.'
The devil you can't sez I!

Many times you've been down on your uppers,
And I've given you coal, sez I,
It's the dirt on me clothes that pays for your ale,
And to that you can testify!

But no matter, I'll take meself off somewhere else.
No more will I come here, sez I.
And I'll tell all me workmates to go elsewhere too
When they have a thirst such as I!

I just hope there's enough fancy folk in this town
To pay for your pretties, sez I.
For it's workmen and dirt, that put you where you are,
As I think you'll recall, by-and-by!

Pauline Hepple

The Beauty Of Nature

I woke up to find a sunny day,
The air smelt sweet with new mown hay.
Looking high across the distant dales,
Such sights of beauty never fails.
To fill my heart with wonder and glee,
Absorbing Mother Nature, surrounding me.
The sky above, a bright clear blue,
Fields of corn in different hue.

Rabbits and deer go scurrying by,
Flocks of lambs, how they jump high.
While walking through the woods I glean,
Birds, trees, and many squirrels are seen.
Collecting together food for their larder,
To sustain them when, the weather gets harder.
For these pleasures and more, I thank God above,
At all the beauty created, by His love.

June F Allum

God's Love Has No Limits

The love of God we clearly can see:-
Just let us stop and look - you and me.
Let's gaze at stars or admire a flower,
These marvels of His love and power.

Out of great love He created them all -
The ants, the birds and the trees so tall;
The atoms, the angels and us too!

Yes, in created things we can trace
The love of God in time and space -
Dearest God, whose love won't let me go -
I truly love you and adore You so!

Could we go through life without seeing
The beauty and purpose of each being?
What a great waste it would all have been
If here on earth God's love we'd never seen!

God's love has no limits known unto man,
Who - out of his mercy and riches
Loves us; again, and again and again -

Zen Rudnicki

The Earl Of Warwick

The barbaric,
Earl of Warwick,
Had a huge red beard,
'I am bold and I am feared,'
He had his portrait painted,
And gave it to those with whom he was acquainted,
Upon seeing it Lady Arabella promptly fainted,
'My Lord is grotesque,'
'With his nose romanesque,'
'And his cheeks increasingly ruddy,'
His ancestors were warlike and bloody,
And he calls Satan his bosom buddy,
His eyes are bloodshot and muddy,
His steed, a trusty pillion,
Matches his beard of red vermilion,
Of men he's killed a million,
And he's never spared a life,
He'll cut out your tongue with a carving knife,
Rumour has it he murdered his very own wife,
In battle he's in the thick of the strife,
He's a disagreeable old curmudgeon,
He'll have you entombed in his dungeon,
With his cudgel he will with you bludgeon,
Thunderous as lightning,
Very, very frightening,
The barbaric,
Earl of Warwick.

Alan Pow

Jesus Christ

I dreamt of an image
It was trying to teach
I reached for its face
It was far out of reach.
It told me a story
Gave truth from the lies
My eyes staring forward
Containing my cries.
It began with a baby
So pure yet so lost
And ends very sadly
For he died on a cross.
His end was the beginning
I could not even speak
As his story unfolded
I could not but weep.
He told of his love
And the healing he done
Of John, Paul, and Mary
He was God's only son.
He reached out and held me
And I just began to say
As he beckoned my silence
Wiped my tears clean away.
He opened his heart
And wrapped me in love
He showed me my saviour
The Lord up above.
Amen.

John Gallagher

This Foxy Lady

This foxy lady has stolen your heart
This foxy lady has taken the part
That is nearest to my heart
That is nearest to my heart

This foxy lady has stolen a dream
She is the cat that gets the cream
She looks at you with those yearning eyes
She won't give up till she gets her prize

With her foxy schemes she'll steal your dreams
When you're gone I'll be missing you
When someone else comes into view
She'll break your heart, break your heart in two

This foxy lady is playing the fool
Like a school kid fresh from school
She'll wreck your dreams and break your heart
Break a promise to a brand new start

This foxy lady has broken the rules
She's like a school kid fresh from school
With her dark brown eyes she can hypnotise
She won't give up 'till she gets her prize.

M J Comley

A Quiet Place

Find me a quiet place,
Far away from this mad, mad race,
My heart is as heavy as the road I tread,
Man has killed the grass,
Planted stone instead.

Where is the boy who tended the sheep?
There are no fields left, where he can sleep.
Man has stolen hay,
For the motorway.

He has poisoned all the rivers,
And polluted God's pure air.
'Moon oh lovely moon, beware'
Find me a quiet place
Far away from this mad, mad race.

A field of flowers, where birds fly free,
And toadstools spring 'neath an old oak tree.
Lush verdant meadows, ever decreasing,
Roads and pollution, ever increasing.

Oh clever man, what is your worth?
Let your children play
And inherit the earth.

Joyce Smith

Little Girl Dancing With Don Jose

His sprightly feet twinkled and tossed in the air,
His black shoes ecstatic, in love with the dance;
A durable courtship, a Spanish affair,
A rose in his bolero, hat all askance.

We danced the carchucha when feet never tarried
Into Alhambra where fountains were falling;
On sounds of wild castanets we were carried
Where scent of herbs from Tarifa were calling.

He promised me as we swept through the paces
We'd dance before Grandees in Alhambra Halls,
Visit Magnolia and Jasmine-sweet places
Where Hoopoe birds quarry; Oleander enthrals.

'Let's dance to Granada my Castillian Don -
You promised to lead where sun is compelling
And the moon and the dance at evening thrive on
By red castle walls where Grandees are dwelling.'

'No, I am an old man and too far from Spain
With strains of Fiesta and lime trees distilling;
The longings that stir in my heart, too, are vain
But dreams and fire of the dance are fulfilling.'

Margret Phillips

The Storm In East Anglia 1936

Slowly, ominously, higher and higher,
Creeps the curtain of lurid and sulphurous fire.
The wind roars, now lulls to a deadly calm,
Then, tears the sky wildly, determined to harm.

The rain, like smoke, in the roaring wind, blowing.
One minute 'tis hailing, the next it is snowing.
The massive trees creak, the drear buildings groan.
The air's filled with wailing and sullen moan.

Hush! - The wind falls - an uncanny stillness reigns over all,
A sense of foreboding, of evil and gall,
Lo! - the sulphur glares and the clouds rift asunder
With a blinding flash and a great crash of thunder.

Uncannier yet, a sheet of blue flame
Rips open the sky and an oak tree doth maim.
The heavens burst open, the angry skies growl
And the thunder rolls on with an ominous howl.

Closer and closer the darkened clouds loom,
Casting o'er all a depressing gloom.
Again and again, in great fury they break,
As the fierce storm strides, with flames in its wake.

A final wrench and the whole sky rends
And a mighty deluge of water descends.
Then - suddenly, there's a ghostly calm.
The storm ends its fury, with no more harm.

The skeletons of trees, in the breathing dark,
Stand gaunt and murky, bleak and stark.
Nature relaxes from the strain
And its whole world is at peace, again.

W R Pettitt